HIGHER EDUCATION
AND SDG4

HIGHER EDUCATION AND THE SUSTAINABLE DEVELOPMENT GOALS

Series Editor

Wendy Purcell, PhD FRSA
Professor with Rutgers University and Academic Research Scholar with Harvard University; Emeritus Professor and University President Emerita.

About the Series

Higher Education and the Sustainable Development Goals is a series of 17 books that address each of the SDGs, in turn, specifically through the lens of higher education. Adopting a solutions-based approach, each book focuses on how higher education is advancing delivery of sustainable development and the United Nations global goals.

Forthcoming Volumes

Higher Education and SDG16: Peace, Justice and Strong Institutions edited by Sarah E. Mendelson

Higher Education and SDG10: Reduced Inequalities edited by Priya Grover, Nidhi Phutela and Pragya Singh

HIGHER EDUCATION AND SDG4

Quality Education

EDITED BY

TAWANA KUPE
Independent Researcher, South Africa

United Kingdom – North America – Japan – India
Malaysia – China

Emerald Publishing Limited
Emerald Publishing, Floor 5, Northspring, 21–23 Wellington Street,
Leeds LS1 4DL.

First edition 2025

Editorial matter and selection © 2025 Tawana Kupe.
Individual chapters © 2025 The authors.
Published under exclusive licence by Emerald Publishing Limited.

Reprints and permissions service
Contact: www.copyright.com

No part of this book may be reproduced, stored in a retrieval system, transmitted in any form or by any means electronic, mechanical, photocopying, recording or otherwise without either the prior written permission of the publisher or a licence permitting restricted copying issued in the UK by The Copyright Licensing Agency and in the USA by The Copyright Clearance Center. No responsibility is accepted for the accuracy of information contained in the text, illustrations or advertisements. The opinions expressed in these chapters are not necessarily those of the Author or the publisher.

British Library Cataloguing in Publication Data
A catalogue record for this book is available from the British Library

ISBN: 978-1-83797-630-0 (Print)
ISBN: 978-1-83797-627-0 (Online)
ISBN: 978-1-83797-629-4 (Epub)

INVESTOR IN PEOPLE

This edited volume is dedicated to my parents Ntihila Kupe and the late William Kupe who were teachers and education administrators dedicated and committed to advancing quality education.

CONTENTS

Series Editor Preface ix

Acknowledgements xiii

Introduction: Setting the Context for Higher Education and SDG 4
Tawana Kupe 1

1. Strategic Partnerships for the Delivery of SDG4 in the Global Education Ecosystem
   Teboho Moja, Lisa Coleman, Monroe France and Palesa Vuyolwethu Tshandu 13

2. Equal Opportunities in Education
   Ramola Ramtohul 35

3. Achieving SDG 4: A Challenge of Education Justice
   Gerald Wangenge-Ouma, Emmanuel Manyasa and Patrick Effiong Ben 55

4. Building Capability for Impact: The Master's in Development Practice at the University of Pretoria
   Samantha Castle, Willem Fourie and Dawie Bornman 75

5. Broadening Engagement and Societal Responsiveness
   Jeffrey Grabill, Simone Buitendijk, Manuel Barcia, and Sonia Kumar 95

6. Conclusion and Way Forward: A Strategic Framework for Higher Education to Achieve SDG 4 Targets
   Brian Chicksen 113

List of Contributors 127

Index 129

SERIES EDITOR PREFACE
Wendy Purcell PhD FRSA, Series Editor

Higher education (HE) makes an important contribution to realising the Sustainable Development Goals (SDGs). Teaching and learning support the development of responsible citizens as scholars, leaders, entrepreneurs and professionals. Curiosity-driven and socially impactful research and innovation help advance knowledge frontiers and find solutions for the world's most pressing issues. As anchor institutions, universities and colleges are also active in civic and community settings, working in partnership with other stakeholders. Given the fierce urgency of (un)sustainable development, the climate crisis and widening inequity within countries and across the globe, HE institutions (HEIs) need to do more and go faster to deliver fully on their potential to help achieve the SDGs.

This book series focuses on the role of HE in advancing the SDGs, identifying some actionable and scalable initiatives and pointing to opportunities ahead. In sharing the ways and means universities and colleges across the world are engaging with the SDGs, the series seeks to both inspire and enable those in the HE sector and stakeholders beyond to transform what they do and how they do it and thereby hasten progress towards Agenda 2030. Insights gleaned from case studies, reflective accounts and student stories can help the HE sector both deepen and accelerate its engagement with the SDGs. Each book seeks to capture examples of how HEIs are fulfilling delivery of their academic mission *and* progressing the SDG concerned. Illustrating the work of students, faculty and staff of the institution, and that undertaken in collaboration with others, positions HE as a change agent operating at a systems level to help create a world that leaves no one behind.

This book focuses on HE and SDG4 'Quality Education' and highlights the work of universities and colleges in achieving this goal to 'ensure inclusive and equitable quality education and promote lifelong learning opportunities for all'. SDG4 is intimately entwined with all the other SDGs and is a key determinant in their delivery, advancing equity and enabling solutions in pursuit of sustainability. A key driver of transformation, HE has the power to change lives and advance a fairer society where everyone can enjoy quality of life. However, the HE ecosystem does not serve everyone and of those it does serve many are not served equitably. Neither is the HE sector optimally situated or HE institutions suitable organised to fully enable the knowledge and human assets they steward and are custodians of to be fully uplifted to realise the SDGs.

Here, the issues, challenges and approaches in amplifying all that is right in the sector and tackling what is wrong with HE are explored as they relate to SDG4. Nascent, emergent and small-scale initiatives seeking to advance sustainable development abound across HE and are testimony to the creativity of students, faculty, staff and leaders. However, efforts to work across disciplinary and/or organisational boundaries within HE or co-creatively with others in business, health systems, civic settings and with other public, private and plural actors are often stymied by competitive or colonial models of education and typically lack the incentives to scale and/or operate over the long term. In addition to other systemic barriers, ranking systems that usefully call out the work of HE in advancing sustainable development can at times diminish innovation with a focus on metrics that lack face validity. So too, professional and statutory bodies involved in accreditation of courses and programmes can interfere with the agile academic innovation needed to tackle the 'polycrisis' encompassed by the SDGs.

Quality education needs to be viewed as an investment in a shared future, not a tax on individual benefits, a future able to meet our needs now without depriving future generations of the same opportunity. However, access to HE is uneven, and only a few of the countries that are signatories to the SDGs are on target to meet SDG4 by 2030. Unemployed and under-employed graduates are an urgent call for HE to refashion itself to better serve the workforce needs of now, those emergent, and others yet unknown. Viewing HE as an ecosystem calls us to connect it more closely with educational pathways for children, youth and adults throughout their life. It invites us to embrace technology to advance access and student success and facilitate more inclusive, personalised and wisdom-led learning journeys. It also prioritises collaboration locally and globally, building connections north to south that seek to tackle education disparities so that human talent is not wasted, and people are enabled to realise their purpose.

Given the central role of quality education to enable people to transform our world at the pace and scale needed, we need to tackle the inequities that plague HE systems. Access to HE without ongoing support to fully realise the actual potential of every person is not acceptable – simply opening the gates to so-called non-traditional learners without setting them up for success is inherently inequitable. Educational justice is explored in this book as central to fostering more equal societies and fundamental to sustainable development. It also highlights new programmes that navigate the theory-practice continuum with HE institutions working locally and globally.

Universities and colleges play a critical role in developing new systemic and transformative solutions through interdisciplinary and multi-stakeholder collaboration and a purposeful focus on the SDGs. As organisations that have stood for many centuries in some cases, this demands that they adapt with new models of learning, research partnerships and leadership and governance frameworks. Immersive engagement with the SDGs can catalyse pedagogic innovation, serve to refresh curricula and stimulate new programme development. It can also open new avenues for research, attract new sources of funding and energise people to deliver on the academic mission.

SDG4 is an enabler of sustainable development and vital to the pursuit of sustainability and the health of people, planet and shared prosperity. This book illustrates this approach with HEIs bringing their key assets of curiosity and the pursuit of knowledge and its application to partners seeking solutions and driving innovation, operating in both local and global networks and connecting the worlds of learning, work and entrepreneurship in support of more sustainable development. Sustainability is a goal for today and sustainable development an organising principle for universities and colleges.

ACKNOWLEDGEMENTS

This book would not have been possible without the efforts of Professor Wendy Purcell, the Series Editor for Emerald Publishing's Sustainable Development Goals series. I am truly grateful to her for nominating me as Editor of this important publication.

I would like to thank several colleagues who assisted and advised me during the process. Firstly, Dr Brian Chicksen, who was the project manager liaising with Professor Purcell and each of the contributing authors at a time when I had an all-consuming job as a Vice Chancellor and Principal. Many thanks go to him for also contributing a chapter.

During the conceptualisation phase, Dr Chicksen worked with a few colleagues at the University of Pretoria who advised on how the book should be framed. These include Professor Irma Eloff, Professor Gerald Wangenge-Ouma, Dr Heide Hackmann, Rikus Delport and Dr Diana Parker.

I spent a few months this year at the University of Montpellier, France, as a Doctoral Honoris Causa fellow. I would like to thank my colleagues from the university for hosting me. In particular, Dr Patrick Carron, the Director of the Montpellier Institute for Advanced Transitions (MAKIT), his colleague Professor Thaura Ghneim-Herrera, the MAKIT administrative staff and the leadership of the university's international division.

Finally, I'd like to thank Ahmed Patel from Media Meme for his invaluable editorial support and superb copy editing. A big thank you to my family, friends and associates for the encouragement and support.

Pretoria, Johannesburg and Montpellier
2024

INTRODUCTION: SETTING THE CONTEXT FOR HIGHER EDUCATION AND SDG 4

Tawana Kupe

Independent Researcher, South Africa

THE GRAND CHALLENGES FACING HUMANITY

From their inception and the commitment by United Nations (UN) member states to their achievement, the Sustainable Development Goals (SDGs) are well recognised as an aspirational framework towards creating a better shared future for all. The 17 SDGs, which are to be attained by 2030, reflect the complexity of the world's challenges. At the same time, they are a call for many institutions across the world to work together to overcome these challenges, which, if left unattended to, will have catastrophic consequences for humanity and the planet.

The SDGs are interrelated and cannot be attained in isolation. SDG 4[1], which is designed to address challenges related to providing quality education, is integral to attaining all the goals. It is, in this sense, a cross-cutting goal and one that requires special attention if we are to expedite development that is inclusive and meaningful.

This book focuses on higher education as a key driver for effectiveness in the sector as a whole. Specifically, it looks at how this effectiveness is largely contingent on providing equal and equitable access to higher education, forming relevant partnerships that bring about transformation in the sector and adopting people-centric approaches that ensure lifelong learning and productive knowledge sharing that leads to sustainable outcomes. This is in the context of (mostly positive) technological disruptions that, if used correctly, has the potential to achieve SDG targets at an exponential rate.

Higher education plays a critical role in shaping broader educational ecosystems at the national, regional and global levels. This includes influencing the direction of education and related policy developments, as well as building the capabilities needed for quality education, from early childhood development all the way up to tertiary education. Higher education is not exempt from the inequalities that persist in society. So, meeting the aspirations of SDG 4 requires intentional reflection and responses to inequality at all stages of the higher education lifecycle. Accordingly, this book will also consider the wide array and different forms of discrimination that drive inequality. In doing so, it offers insights and interventions that should make a difference.

Tertiary institutions exist in a complex, disrupted, uncertain and globally connected landscape. Despite the many threats they face, there are also opportunities for them across political, economic, social, technological, legal and environmental domains and ecosystems. Not only are challenges discrete within these ecosystems, but there exist multiple interfaces, interdependencies and feedback loops between them. Shocks and dramatic changes to circumstances are frequent and inevitable, such that we no longer speak of a 'new normal' but are coming to understand a 'new unusual', which is dynamic and uncertain.

The manifestation and implications of our landscape dynamics are myriad, and only a few will be highlighted here. Conflicts and wars that are raging in countries and regions across the world are evidence of a broader conflict that has a global footprint. The essence of the latter lies in the desire to solve differences, mostly through violence, to serve only narrow interests. The very global dimension that this violence assumes is very much rooted in underdevelopment at the community and individual levels.

Rising populism, corruption, misinformation and disinformation are commonly associated with the rejection of science and the facts that arise from it. Where knowledge is valued, it is often ring-fenced through mechanisms such as pay walls and unfair pricing to benefit only a few. This is often protected through nationalistic and competing agendas. Democratic systems and fair global rule making are under severe stress, and the many fault lines in global economic systems are preventing just, inclusive, equitable and sustainable development. As a result, issues of poverty, inequality and unemployment persist and remain ubiquitous.

Technological advancements that are mainly, if not exclusively, digital present a plethora of opportunities to influence models of education and access thereof. But paradoxically, these opportunities are left untapped because the high costs of technology prevent equal access and only serve to deepen the digital divide. Even within the context of pursuing the attainment of the SDGs, there is increasing recognition of resource scarcity and how development itself impacts negatively on the environment, especially in terms of climate change.

In this complex milieu, deficiencies in the higher education sector are profound and are made clear in the way its macrosystemic structures are configured. Pervasive and entrenched inaccessibility and inequalities that are related to resourcing and capabilities underscore these configurations. While universities are perfectly placed to create spaces for dialogue, where multiple voices can contribute to the understanding of the problems we face as well as begin to create the necessary solutions as a collective, we are currently not fully positioned to fulfil this role. At the same time, our very existence is under threat. As societal stakeholders are increasingly questioning the exclusivity of universities, their perceived dislocation/alienation from societal needs and their contributions to advancing sustainable futures, there is a crisis of funding (whether by the state or the private sector) for public institutions.

Another harsh reality that we face while trying to respond to these challenges is that we do not have the luxury of time to save the planet. We may speak of a commitment towards 2030, but we are already immersed in a storm seems unlikely to abate by then. So, when we think of the future, we must remember Neil LaBute's famous words: 'The future is now. It's time to grow up and be strong. Tomorrow may well be too late'. We should also keep in mind the words of Chief Albert Luthuli, the first Nobel Laureate from Africa: 'The test is action'. We should not, therefore, theorise interminably, procrastinate or limit access to knowledge.

As we introspect and chart our way forward, the time for action is now, and while our actions must be considered and inclusive, they must also be swift. They must be accompanied by a preparedness to champion a cause that we and the world we share depend on. Transformational and intentional leadership is the call of the hour.

A REIMAGINED ROLE OF UNIVERSITIES AS AGENTS FOR THE PUBLIC GOOD

A good starting point is to reimagine the role of universities in society. Institutions of higher learning exist because of society, and it follows that they should function for the good of society. It is their duty, then, to ensure and expand their relevance and increase their efforts to be more impactful in society. This should be characterised by inclusivity and clear contributions to just, inclusive and sustainable development. Through its collaborative design and aspirational outlook, SDG 4 provides the higher education sector with an adequate and acceptable framework to shape its actions in a way that is relevant to society. The question is not whether the sector will attain the goals but what is does to achieve them.

In a reimagined role, higher education institutions are for the public good. Ensuring this would mean responding to Chris Brink's incisive commentary in 'The Soul of a University', where he contends that we should not ask 'What are we good at?' but 'What are we good for?'. In response to this overarching question, it suffices to say that what society needs from higher education are institutions that embrace excellence and strive to be relevant and effective in the pursuit of fundamental knowledge and challenge-led research. The higher education sector, in this sense, needs to leverage its strengths and capabilities to demonstrate responsiveness to the contexts in which it is embedded. As a collective, players in the sector must value and embrace collaboration to fully respond to and deliver on the needs of society. Overall, there must be a restoration of trust in higher education and research, and strengthening of the pact between universities, the state, the private sector and civil society.

Such a proposition is neither philanthropic nor a 'nice to have'. Rather, it serves to point out that means of collaboration within and among universities must change at a rapid pace. There are increasing expectations for universities to demonstrate their relevance in society. These expectations inadvertently compel them to adequately respond to the 'wicked' and grand challenges facing humanity. To do this, they must shift from solely generating knowledge to translating that knowledge into meaningful and effective solutions. This is why open knowledge systems matter, because in such systems the traditional, silo-driven approach is abandoned for more inclusive, and ultimately more enriching, approaches to higher education.

In essence, SDG 4 emphasises the importance of innovation when it comes to how institutions are organised. The targeted outcomes of the goal, therefore, encourage an innovative shift away from rigidly focusing on the efficient management of dwindling resources, as well as pandering to those who demand more training and less education that supports and upholds democratic values and principles. This reimagined university will be involved in a double act of transforming itself and the society in which it operates. When put together, the SDGs are about fundamentally transforming society to achieve sustainability. Without accepting and participating fully in this double act, the university's credibility and legitimacy as a transformative agent will be questioned and its impact will be blunted.

The transformed university of the future will be in touch with societal needs and will thrive off its ability to collaborate within itself and across its boundaries. It will be a university that is defined by its broad, inclusive and forward-looking approaches and being connected to its peers and other stakeholders. Ultimately, it will be a university that at its core promotes mutual benefit and empowerment in the interests of the public good. This 'next generation' university will also be future literate, that is, it will be able to suspend pre-existing mental models and paradigms to envisage the future in different and unconstrained ways. Relevant and truly innovative solutions will flow as talent is unearthed and used productively to realise multiple streams of value.

CREATING LEVERAGE IN THE REIMAGINED UNIVERSITY

Within a value network of peers and stakeholders, the reimagined university functions as a system and as a set of interrelated systems. A major source of leverage in this situation is advancing transdisciplinarity, which in its true and full meaning must include engaged scholarship. It involves the ability to collaborate across different disciplines, fields of knowledge and sectors around complex, real-world problems. Its underlying intention is to find and co-create meaningful societal solutions that expand the life chances of those who are most in need. This means embracing and valuing all forms of validated knowledge and expertise – from the embedded knowledge of 'street experts' to the formal, celebrated and peer-reviewed experts that we know.

Two fundamental dimensions are important in this setting – the nature of relationships and engagement, and the nature of knowledge and solutions. Engagement within relationships may be underpinned by either low or high levels of trust. Knowledge and solutions may be protected or may be open and accessible. Where there are low levels of trust and where knowledge is protected, we find ourselves in a transactional space characterised by silos, the pursuit of personal interests that often lead to dysfunction and absolute outcomes that are aimed at creating winners and losers. This low-trust, protected model is unlikely to adequately address the complex challenges that we face. We should rather seek the opposite, which is a transformed and transformational space of engaged responsiveness characterised by high levels of trust, and open and innovative knowledge-sharing. In this more productive situation, knowledge is very likely to be translated into solutions that make a difference in a truly accelerated way.

In moving from transactional silos to engaged responsiveness, higher education institutions will, as a matter of course, adopt a two-pronged approach. This entails changing the way it nurtures and strengthens trust-based relationships, and the way knowledge is generated and used. Trust-based relationships are underpinned by a shared understanding and common purpose among stakeholders across the higher education value chain. They have the same commitment to co-designing and co-creating solutions for the public good. Embedded in this new paradigm is a compelling case for open data, science and education. To this end, there is effective knowledge-sharing, a mutual valuing of different sources of knowledge and talent, building broad-based and even capabilities to address challenges and capitalise on opportunities.

ENGAGED RESPONSIVENESS THROUGH COLLABORATION: BARRIERS AND OPPORTUNITIES

There are clear barriers to realise this aspiration. The imbalances that exist within global education ecosystems, such as the vast disparities between institutions in the Global North and the Global South, inevitably create powerful resistance to change. In this context, those who have remain content in their comfort, while the voice of those who have not holds little sway and is easily dismissed.

Current paradigms of unequal advantages are somewhat reinforced by the many university ranking systems. This is shown by how siloed and anti-collaborative institutional cultures have become to participate in them. The cycle becomes more difficult to disrupt because the criteria for ranking high on these systems often speak to the extent to which universities are siloed.

In reflecting critically on the higher education system, we must also recognise that the system itself has evolved from being concerned purely with specialisation to one that, through its rigid focus on specialisation, reinforces rather than alleviates inequalities. This recognition is necessary when attempting to push the frontiers of disciplinary knowledge. However, there is still much work to do in the way of retaining disciplinary excellence while transcending limited disciplinary focus towards connecting and collaborating across diverse fields of knowledge and interest. Only once this is achieved will higher education be able to drive meaningful change and shift societal dynamics in fundamental and sustainable ways.

The metrics that are currently being used to measure success and impact are flawed. This is because they fall short when critically assessing our involvement in societal transformation. At best, indicators such as research output and productivity, the quality of the journals that academics publish in and citation counts only feed into performance assessments in a low-trust, protected academic ecosystem. These outputs, important as they are, should be a means to an end and not an end in themselves. In isolation, they are weak surrogates for the impact that universities should be making. For example, at macro-societal levels, universities should be involved in addressing poverty and inequality, while at micro-societal levels, they should enhance the lives of people and the communities that they live in. Such impact is not easily measured by extant academic metrics.

A STRATEGIC APPROACH TO NAVIGATING DYNAMICS, ADDRESSING BARRIERS AND TAKING OPPORTUNITIES

A next-generation university is one that embraces collaboration and openness. The challenge in developing strategies that promote this lies in crafting new approaches to operating within varied but interrelated ecosystems (these include the politico-legal, economic, social and biophysical spheres of society). Ecosystem resilience should be central to this new approach, which would inadvertently be given expression through the meaningful existence of people and the societies in which they live.

But there are certain prerequisites for responding effectively to the challenge. At the outset, universities must demonstrate focused transformational leadership, individually and collectively, across the higher education sector. This is the type of leadership that is in touch with society, is resolute in upholding and promoting basic human rights and is devoted to unlocking human potential that serves the greater good. Such leaders are also mindful of the impact of human development on the environment and embrace co-existence with all forms of life.

Once there is visible and felt leadership, universities must play a critical role in securing a just and sustainable future for the world. This would entail leveraging the growing expectations from society that universities will play a role in change for the better. This should, in turn, enable a positive shift in the dynamics at play in global education ecosystems. Through this shift, we will become more capable of influencing the configuration of the politico-legal, economic, social and biophysical spheres that operate within a broader ecosystem.

Individual leaders and universities acting independently and in isolation cannot bring about this kind of structural change. Rather, there is a need to establish and strengthen 'a coalition of the willing' that serves as a catalyst for change. Progressively increasing the size and influence of this coalition has the potential to reach a critical mass from which a new set of paradigms and standards for higher education emerges.

Such change cannot happen if a transdisciplinary and collaborative agenda is not advanced. A key part of this agenda is an established yet fluid futures literacy that is anchored in transdisciplinary excellence. Our collaborative effort must also recognise the connection between macro-ecosystem renewal and the positive gains made by individuals and communities on the micro level.

Collaborative efforts should result in strengthened and mutually empowered institutions and collaborators and partners. This entails building a new paradigm of partnerships and collaborations that are not just bilateral but multilateral and transcend the disparities between the Global North and the Global South. These relationships should, therefore, be centred on equity and mutual benefit mutual empowerment. A wide range of collaborations is possible across teaching, learning, research, engagement and outreach. Key factors of this include pursuing decolonial modes of teaching and research, the ability to work within and across physical and virtual platforms (i.e. multimodal mobility), global classrooms and using education and research to intentionally address the challenges that hinder sustainable social and environmental justice. All forms of knowledge must be accessible in this new paradigm, which must then be translated into real change, accelerated innovation and positive experiences. Higher education institutions should learn from each other and rapidly adapt their acquired knowledge to different contexts.

This new approach must be explored further to determine how it could be effectively implemented. It includes mobilising diverse stakeholders around a particular issue, sharing different perspectives and developing a common understanding of the problem with its related issues and co-designing solutions. A basket of qualitative and quantitative success indicators should be identified across social, economic and environmental dimensions. Demonstrating impact with new and relevant sets of metrics, as seen by ecosystem renewal and through the eyes of partners, recipients and society at large (e.g. by structuring a series of focus group conversations) will create a virtuous cycle of change, learning and impact.

INTRODUCING THE CHAPTERS

Chapter 1: Strategic Partnerships for the Delivery of SDG4 in the Global Education Ecosystem

By Teboho Moja, lead author (New York University/University of Pretoria); Lisa Coleman (New York University); Monroe France (Tufts University); Palesa Vuyolethu Tshandu (New York University)

In this chapter, the authors explore recent developments, challenges, opportunities and strategic initiatives relating to higher education systems. This exploration is done through the lens of higher education as a catalyst for social transformation, economic diversification and sustainable development, including the development of strategic and equitable global partnerships. Challenges, which include limited access, under-preparedness and lack of funding for students to pursue studies outside their own countries, are brought to the fore and discussed. Opportunities and strategic initiatives for delivering on quality education and societal transformation are also discussed. This is done by highlighting the role of effective partnerships and the connection between SDG 4 and the other SDGs.

Chapter 2: Equal Opportunities in Education

By Ramola Ramtohul

The principal dimensions of inequality in the higher education sector that hinder the attainment of SDG 4 are discussed in this chapter. Using a wide-angle lens, the author examines the key underlying factors that drive inequality in education, inequality across the education lifecycle and the special characteristics of discrimination. Strategies that can help reduce inequalities in the higher education sector are also explored.

Chapter 3: Achieving SDG 4: A Challenge of Education Justice

By Gerald Wangenge-Ouma, Emmanuel Manyasa and Patrick Effiong Ben

Drawing on the nexus between education justice in basic and higher education, this chapter exposes the nature of the challenges that sustain the injustices of educational exclusion and poor-quality education. The authors argue that SDG 4 targets cannot be achieved without education justice, which entails that every child, young person and adult benefit from quality education and lifelong learning. Accordingly, the authors discuss how SDG 4 can be attained by tackling the problem of social, political and economic exclusion that emerges from the higher education sector.

Chapter 4: Building Capability for Impact: The Master's in Development Practice at the University of Pretoria

By Samantha Castle, Willem Fourie and Dawie Bornman

The authors discuss the development of a Master's in Development Practice (MDP) degree programme at the University of Pretoria. The programme's affiliation to the Global Association of MDP is used as a case study to illustrate how this explicitly multidisciplinary programme can support the development of leadership capabilities that are needed to achieve the SDGs. The chapter includes theoretical perspectives as well reflections from a course supervisor and a student who participated in the programme.

Chapter 5: Broadening Engagement and Societal Responsiveness

By Jeffrey Grabill and Simone Buitendijk

This chapter looks at how universities may increase their efforts to meaningfully contribute to resolving the major societal issues of today. The fundamental question here hinges on whether universities can ensure and increase their relevance in a way that is ethically and socially responsible. By using the engagement and social responsibility policies of universities in the UK and the USA as examples, the authors offer a pragmatic approach that might respond to this question adequately. In doing so, they encourage stakeholders in the higher education sector to 'think differently'.

Chapter 6: Conclusion and Way Forward: A Strategic Framework for Higher Education to Achieve SDG 4 Targets

By Brian Chicksen

Achieving targets within SDG 4 is key to successfully achieving all the goals within the SDG framework. In this chapter, the role of higher education in attaining Sustainable Development Goal (SDG) 4 is discussed in relation to achieving the other 16 SDGs. This is done by reflecting on the prevailing and anticipated challenges and opportunities faced by the higher education sector and proposing a strategic framework to enable realisation of its full potential. A design-thinking approach to formulating strategy is used.

NOTE

1. The full title of SDG 4 is: 'Ensure inclusive and equitable quality education and promote lifelong learning opportunities for all.' For more information about SDG 4 and its targets, visit: https://sdgs.un.org/goals/goal4

1

STRATEGIC PARTNERSHIPS FOR THE DELIVERY OF SDG4 IN THE GLOBAL EDUCATION ECOSYSTEM

Teboho Moja[a,b], Lisa Coleman[d], Monroe France[c] and Palesa Vuyolwethu Tshandu[a]

[a]New York University, USA
[b]University of Pretoria, USA
[c]Tufts University, USA
[d]Adler University, USA

ABSTRACT

This chapter explores recent developments, challenges, opportunities and strategic initiatives in higher education systems. These systems can be seen as catalysts for social transformation, economic diversification and sustainable development. This includes developing strategic and equitable global partnerships and collaboration. In this chapter, the authors discuss challenges such as limited access, being underprepared and a lack of funding that is necessary for students to pursue studies outside of their own countries. The authors also discuss opportunities and strategic initiatives for delivering on quality education and social transformation. This is done by highlighting the role of effective partnerships and the connection between Sustainable Development Goal (SDG) 4 and the other SDGs. Using education policy and its subsequent implementation, the authors frame their discussions on educational reform to acknowledge the impact of higher education across multiple dimensions. The chapter concludes with student perspectives on the issues raised and a deeper consideration of some challenges they face in pursuit of quality higher education.

Keywords: Affordability; digitisation; partnerships; social transformation; strategic initiatives; sustainability

INTRODUCTION

Higher education is a critical component of the global education ecosystem. It is one that largely determines the achievement of the SDGs. It is central to SDG 4, which, among its seven outcomes, targets equal access to affordable, high-quality education opportunities and lifelong learning (UNESCO, n.d.a.). Higher education is recognised globally as an important factor in shaping society and as a catalyst to transformation and development. According to UNESCO, higher education 'enables personal development and promotes economic, technological and social change' (UNESCO, 2023a, para. 2). Diversification in higher education is also vitally important for sociocultural and economic development and for equipping younger generations with skills, knowledge and ideals for the future.

At a macrosystemic level, imbalances in education ecosystems across the world persist. These include vast disparities between those in the Global North and Global South. The developmental trajectories of many nation-states are also varied, and certain measures are required to ensure coordination and cooperation across and between various sectors, including technical, professional, secondary and post-secondary institutions. At the same time, new opportunities, particularly in the technology domain, are improving how knowledge can be produced, managed, distributed and acted on at all levels of the education system. This makes it necessary to understand and confront antiquated and inequitable policies towards designing ones that leverage new opportunities and codify participation with the aim of meeting SDG 4 targets.

SDG 4 AND THE GLOBAL EDUCATION ECOSYSTEM

Higher education has been the catalyst for how we have thought about and structured societies. Major reforms in education systems across the world have taken place in the previous and current centuries. Reforms in higher education have shaped and facilitated the formation of contemporary society, catalysed social and professional mobilisation and created new forms of the economy (Schofer et al., 2020). They also state that central features of modern global societies rely on the 'distinctive form of higher education' (p. 1) that has been integrated into societies across the world. According to Hill et al. (2005), regions with a highly educated workforce, and where large investments have been made in their higher education systems, have higher wages for all workers and exponential growth in prosperity.

UNESCO has indicated its desire to 'ensure that all learners [on a global scale] acquire the knowledge and skills needed to promote sustainable development [through education]' by 2030 (United Nations, 2015, Target 4.7). As such, higher education is critical in advancing the SDGs generally and SDG 4 in particular.

Achieving the SDG 4 targets, which are set to 'ensure inclusive and equitable quality education and promote lifelong learning opportunities for all' (UNESCO. n.d., Definition section), is certainly daunting. These targets are 'pivotal [to] positive change, emphasising the transformative power of education in fostering a sustainable and equitable world' (UNESCO, n.d., Definition section). Crucial pathways to attain these targets are outlined in seven outcomes, which are:

- Universal primary and secondary education;
- Early childhood development and universal pre-primary education;
- Equal access to technical/vocational and higher education;
- Relevant skills for decent work;
- Gender equality and inclusion;
- Universal youth literacy; and
- Education for sustainable development and global citizenship.

UNESCO provides three means of implementation to meet the targets and achieve these outcomes:

- Creating effective learning environments;
- Providing scholarships; and
- Increasing the supply of qualified teachers.

SDG 4 was formulated with the aim of addressing various challenges within the global education ecosystem. It recognises that achieving universal access on its own is insufficient without ensuring that the education offered is of high quality and results in quality learning outcomes. In this regard, SDG 4 is a critical driver for sustainable development in several areas beyond the global education ecosystem. These include economic growth, social inclusion and environmental sustainability. Focusing on SDG 4 enables the achievement and success of other SDGs as they are interconnected and interdependent. As such, they cannot be achieved by working in silos.

For example, SDG 9 focuses on building resilient infrastructure and promoting innovation and inclusive industrial markets. For this to be achieved, we need higher education programmes that are developed in partnership with industry players to bridge skills gaps. There are also links between SDG 4 and SDGs 5 and 10, which deal with gender equality and empowerment, and reducing inequalities within and among countries, respectively. Similarly, SDG 3, which involves promoting healthy lives and wellbeing, recognises the role of education in promoting health awareness. SDG 8, whose targets are set around promoting economic growth, employment and decent work for all, emphasises the connection between education and economic development.

To make progress towards achieving SDG 4 and advancing the other goals, systems need to offer inclusive and equitable education, acknowledge and address the diverse needs of learners, including those from marginalised groups. There must also be awareness of changes in the learning and working environments that inform the needs of emerging markets. These include cultural and environmental changes and identity shifts (e.g. in gender and sexual orientation), technological disruptions such as artificial intelligence (AI), robotics, machine learning and cybersecurity as well as developments in social and political landscapes. For this awareness to lead to action, educators and policymakers need to be innovative and collaborate with various sectors to ensure that students are prepared to solve world problems and work within new and emerging markets.

Recognition must also be given to the need for learners to gain knowledge and develop the skills necessary to become nimble to meet the ever-changing demands of the global economy. This applies particularly to the fast-changing technology and information sectors. Castells (2004) refers to the 'programmable and self-programmable workforce' in making the distinction between learners who can do 'generic' labour (considered 'disposable' and 'easily replaceable') and those with the creative capacity to autonomously synthesise information from varied and increasingly complex sources.

The task to transform society is too daunting to be achieved by one sector alone or through one goal. In response to this, SDG 17 calls for the fostering of global partnerships to play a role in achieving social transformation and requires the development of strategies relevant and suitable for different regional needs. As such, this SDG encourages partnerships between the education and other sectors. Moja (2018) asserts the importance of exploring and promoting regional collaboration through various forms of partnerships and projects that drive innovation in teaching, research and community engagement. This approach is necessary to achieve better higher education outcomes, especially when faced with increased internationalisation (Cloete et al., 2004).

If structured well, increased global partnerships have the potential to play a part in responding to the issue of unevenness and imbalances among educational ecosystems, including the vast disparities between the Global North and Global South. In this sense, the importance of cross-country and multi-institutional partnerships is essential for bringing together the best minds to tackle various global challenges such as ending poverty (as articulated in SDG 1) and access to clean water and sanitation (as articulated in SDG 6).

In the following sections, we share a snapshot of developments and challenges in education. This is done by providing examples of successful programmes, partnerships and policies designed to strengthen relationships with governments, advance research and innovation, promote interdisciplinary collaboration, enhance industry–academia partnerships and foster social entrepreneurship. In doing so, we aim to illustrate various ways in which higher education has the power to bridge workforce gaps, develop inclusive leaders, contribute to community and civic engagement and help respond social challenges.

RECENT DEVELOPMENTS AND CHALLENGES IN THE GLOBAL EDUCATION ECOSYSTEM

Over the past 15 years, the global education ecosystem has faced several challenges. These include rising concerns around technological developments such as AI, climate change and its relationship to education, leadership shifts, decolonising curriculums, the future of work, democratising employment processes and how we define education and learning. Additional issues related to global inclusion, research production, diversity, equity and access across the gender, race, ethnic and other demographic strata have also been of concern. As internal, domestic and geopolitical demographic shifts occur, so should the work of higher education institutions to navigate increasing volatility, uncertainty, complexity and ambiguity (Bennett & Lemoine, 2014).

These issues are further exacerbated by the number of students who graduate but are considered underprepared to meet workforce needs on a regional or global scale, including the needs of emerging industries. This challenge has led to large numbers of unemployed or underemployed graduates, which translates into wasted resources and unpaid student loans. This likely stems from students who are admitted into higher education institutions but are underprepared, which negatively impacts higher education outcomes.

For innovation and social transformation to occur, learners need to have access to quality education in all respects, from entry to exit, including the transition from the higher education system to the workforce. In addition to addressing the issue of an underfunded higher education system, educators and policymakers need to also think about meeting a growing demand due to population growth and expectations of increased social mobility.

The global economic system is increasingly dependent on and driven by access to information and the production of knowledge. While higher education is well positioned to provide this, there is limited capacity to do so as many institutions are hampered by low levels of access to research funding. This is particularly the case for institutions in the Global South. To give us an idea of disparities in this regard, 86% of research publications in 2022 were from developed regions, countries or economies (Schneider et al., 2023). This highlights the level of inequality when it comes to accessing, producing and using advanced knowledge and research.

Major predictions for radical change in higher education were made at the turn of the century, mainly due to the rapid advancement and application of ICT across sectors. Digital transformation was further accelerated by the COVID-19 pandemic, which accelerated investments in digital infrastructure by governments and institutions to keep up with the delivery of remote education and other essential services.

In response to the emergence of generative AI and its use in education, UNESCO's unit for technology and AI in education, future of learning and innovation released a 'Guidance for generative AI in education and research'. While recognising the development potential of these technologies, the guidelines provide a framework to respond to the challenges they pose, which include the perpetuation of biases and risks if left unregulated. This initiative builds on UNESCO's prior recommendations and emphasises the importance of equity and diverse cultural representation in relation to generative AI (UNESCO, 2023b). These issues are also connected to SDG 5, which focuses on achieving gender equality and empowerment.

Even with major education reforms and a substantial increase in enrolments across the world, access to higher education is uneven. For example, in sub-Saharan Africa, an average annual increase of 8.4% in enrolments in higher education institutions has been recorded. This outpaces growth rates in the USA and other Western countries (Chien & Chiteng, 2012). Yet less than 10% of graduates in the region report feeling prepared for the future (UNESCO, 2022).

There is a need for major shifts in global government practices and social reforms, and greater emphasis on addressing access to higher education. This should be done to address the persistent gaps that leave millions of young people without skills that would open employment opportunities. For this to happen, education policy and practice need to be reformed. Educators and policymakers understand the varying local and global factors that perpetuate barriers to access, including various geopolitical conflicts and global crises. As such, they need to provide funds for sustainable interventions and develop sustainable strategies. They must also be sensitive to and skilled at navigating these barriers in terms of impact on student success outcomes, including those that correlate with greater preparedness for the global workforce and the needs of emerging industries (Clark et al., 2023).

To be effective, SDG 4 needs to be linked with other SDGs for an intentional uplift and positive shift towards transdisciplinary scholarship. Access, traditional models, single disciplinarity and physical learning spaces are among some of the challenging areas to be reformed in the higher education ecosystem (Chatlani, 2018). The higher education market also continues to face disruptions that have caused schools to shut down programmes, close completely or consolidate programmes or merge colleges (Higher Ed Dive Team, 2023). Due to the complex nature of these challenges, work to achieve the SDG 4 targets requires innovative approaches to strategy and practice. This calls for re-evaluating purpose, developing long-term strategies, inculcating multifaceted practices that involve co-creation and using research and technological interventions in newly and collectively imagined ways.

RETHINKING PARTNERSHIPS TO ACHIEVE SDG 4 TARGETS

To respond to and achieve the targets set in SDG 4, multisectoral and globally diverse partnerships need to be reimagined. New forms of partnership are needed to address challenges related to the future of work, technological shifts, accessibility and digital divides that continue to haunt the global higher education landscape. It is projected that only one in six countries will achieve the SDG 4 targets by 2030 (United Nations, n.d.). Continued attention to Eurocentric approaches to global education challenges perpetuates ineffective outcomes in bridging educational gaps and realising outcomes. As such, a deliberate focus on building-specific strategic interventions to reimagine global higher education programmes is necessary to successfully navigate these and other emerging challenges.

For most of the history of education, many international and partnership-developed programmes have been concentrated in Europe. As many colleges and universities in the USA expanded, their programmes were established and centred in partnering with Europe, with some in the Middle East, albeit limited. In addition, given the partnership of Eurocentric faculties in the USA, studies have mostly been focused in and on the West. Even the relatively few ancillary studies of countries characterised as 'developing' were conducted through a Eurocentric lens. Although partnership programmes have been established outside of Europe, in many of these partnerships, there is little evidence of structures, principles and practices that are not Eurocentric. As such, the dominant, Eurocentric, university determines and reinforces the structures for partnership, while the less dominant partner is left with limited power to negotiate, create relevant research or challenge practices that follow colonial patterns. This renders these partnerships irrelevant globally as they are not truly co-created and do not prioritise reciprocity or equity.

This pattern of partnership expansion is neither new in the education ecosystem nor to the way bilateral partnerships have operated historically. As Eurocentric education is built on methods derived from colonial interests, studying abroad, especially in short-term programmes, often meant that only those with privilege and economic advantage were able to go and study the 'other' existing outside of the European context. There are still echoes of these former colonial patterns in the current practices Western-based programmes. These practices are institutionalised by means of complicated structures and canonical foundations based on European traditions. As a result, many international programmes that started in the USA follow the pattern of cultivating unequal power relations and partnerships, which foster unequal outcomes that perpetuate inequitable results instead of creating innovative global educational pathways.

To begin reimagining international partnerships, colonial legacies in the global higher education ecosystem need to be rooted out. This will entail inclusive processes of strategic restructuring. To do so, global partners together with their intended beneficiaries need to identify clear and achievable goals that are reciprocal in learning philosophies, processes and outcomes. For example, access to quality science, technology, engineering and mathematics (STEM) education for many women in European countries have been limited due to ongoing biases and other factors. While women are achieving some access to education in the West, there is a great deal of variation, which impacts on employment for women globally (Microsoft. 2017).

Conversely, in many Muslim-majority countries, there are more women engineers than men. For example, in Iran, 70% of university graduates in STEM are women. In the United Arab Emirates, Oman and Saudi Arabia, 60% of STEM graduates are women (Weingarten, 2017). In the same article, Weingarten (2017) is quoted as saying:

> *The West has invested billions of dollars to address the issue of gender inequality in engineering and computing and has basically failed ... I started thinking maybe we're asking the wrong questions – questions that won't help us solve the problem (para. 4).*

In addition, we might not be looking at countries that have the solutions and strategies we need to explore.

The dominant representation, philosophical modelling and policies of Western universities are a perpetual cycle in the overall design of higher education. It often does not allow for reciprocity in global partnerships across higher education. Yarmoshuk et al. (2020) observed that:

> *Interuniversity global health partnerships are often between parties unequal in organisational capacity and performance using conventional academic output measures ... Asymmetry of partners, dissimilar perspectives and priorities, and terms of funding all pose challenges to reciprocity. In an era when strengthening institutions is considered*

> crucial to achieving development goals, more rigorous examination and assessment of reciprocity in partnerships is warranted. (Yarmoshuk et al., 2020, Abstract section)

Strategic partnerships built in reciprocity might prove beneficial in realising the SDG 4 target areas. For example, Sors et al. (2023) highlight an international partnership – described by them as a reciprocal innovation – between the USA and Kenya spanning three decades. In the same article, they expand on the meaning of the term: 'Reciprocal innovation harnesses a bidirectional, co-constituted and iterative exchange of ideas, resources and innovations to address shared health challenges across diverse global settings' (Sors et al., 2023, Abstract section). The partnership included activities such as hosting the annual meetings of multinational researchers and practitioners for learning and support to the programme, as well as transferring lessons learnt from Kenya to the USA (Sors et al., 2023).

By employing such intentional reciprocity based on innovation and design thinking, Western researchers and practitioners might learn something about alternative bodies of knowledge such as indigenous knowledge systems and resolving gender disparities in science systems through engaging in co-created global partnership initiatives. These types of reciprocity-based strategic actions might not only help leverage and maximise lessons about women in education but also allow for the application of those lessons to employment to address gender disparities.

Another area that might benefit from reciprocity-based partnerships is youth literacy (general and digital) in the context of a persistent digital divide. Library partnerships and digital platforms designed and reimagined by young people across the world are crucial. For example, platforms built by young people through processes of co-creation that focus on literacy and access to bridge digital divides might be supported through multifaceted and multisectoral industry partnerships. One of the key lessons learnt from the COVID-19 pandemic is that we have greater capacity to become more closely connected, often through virtual and digital platforms. Companies had to work together to address health crises globally. Specifically, young people across the world are more connected now than ever before. Leveraging these connections might initiate a similar process, where the industry engages in intergenerational partnerships and co-learning to address literary gaps (UNDESA, n.d.a).

There is a great deal of evidence that demonstrates bias in emerging technologies related to ethnicity, gender and other salient identity factors (Noble, 2018). However, global partnerships that are diverse and intergenerational are likely to result in these technologies becoming more inclusive, for example, co-created algorithms (Silberg & Manyika, 2019).

A reimagining of expertise and the redefinition of expertise to be inclusive are also needed to realise SDG 4 targets. Processes of co-creation are key to doing this. This ties in to strengthening and leveraging intergenerational partnerships and connections, as well as decentring the colonial narrative by promoting a people- and planet-centred approach to educational development. This approach is, in turn, well positioned to find pathways to addressing challenges such as access to education, clean water, healthcare and income generation (Korten, 1987; Ministry of Foreign Affairs of Japan, 1996; United Nations, 2023). This reimagined approach is also directly related to the other SDGs such as SDG 3 (health) and SDG 6 (water and sanitation).

Co-creation and decolonised education will involve not only challenging the Eurocentric practices that have influenced education but recognising and uprooting those practices that are still present. According to Zavala (2016):

> *Decolonial methodologies in education need to be repositioned and situated within broader geographic-historical processes. Specifically, a broader framework for community development and the self-determination of colonised peoples ensures that decolonial practices are defined relationally rather than by a set of essential qualities. Decolonial education is a process for ... self-determination and for reimagining what is centred as knowledge and expertise (p. 1).*

Engaging new processes for research activities, as well as for teachers and learners in globally divergent and decolonial practices is, in this sense, essential to rethinking how expertise could be more effectively used for planet-centred research and policy development. Research partnerships generated from and built through reciprocity can also begin the process of decolonising technology and ways of approaching climate issues, among others.

To achieve the SDG 4 targets – particularly in terms of equal access to technical, vocational and higher education – work opportunities not only must be created through reciprocal partnerships but also should be motivated by a dedication to continuous learning beyond the typical years. Framing the postcolonial learning process as ongoing would foreground skills enhancement and development, which, in turn, would lead to an overall enhancement of learning in the workplace. UNESCO's Global Education Monitoring Report notes the following:

> *Over 60 million secondary students worldwide were enrolled in technical and vocational education in 2015 – about 10% of all secondary students – mostly at the upper secondary level. Most regions had seen little change in this rate since 2000, although participation rose in the Caucasus and Central Asia and fell in the Pacific. Technical and vocational education remained male-dominated, with girls accounting for 43% of enrolment. In 2015, 213 million students were enrolled in tertiary education. Since 2000, the gross enrolment ratio has risen by almost 30 percentage points in upper middle-income countries, from 17% to 46%. However, enrolment growth in the Caucasus, Central Asia and sub-Saharan Africa almost stagnated. The share of private enrolment has been increasing. Women have outpaced men in tertiary enrolment, with sub-Saharan Africa the only region where fewer women than men enrol.*
> *(UNESCO, n.d.b, para. 2–3)*

These statistics highlight the importance of focusing on lifelong education as it pertains to present and future employment opportunities and holds relevance to redressing gender disparities.

New approaches to adult education will help improve global literacy rates, as has been demonstrated in Canada through the Canada West Foundation (Lane & Murray, 2018). Revitalising and re-engaging adults through educational opportunities will improve work outcomes and employment gaps. They can also help in 'cultivating contexts where adult educators can become change agents who recognise that the individual and community are intricately entangled'. This 'demands that educators grow new capacities, make new tools, develop thicker networks, and cultivate intentional links among each other to foster ecologies of transformation, and ecological environments' that are based in collaboration and co-creation (Nicolaides et al., 2024).

The West's preoccupation with education for the 17–23 age group has dominated higher education practices. A shift towards lifelong learning that is designed to engage 'adult learners' is critical. In their 2019 article, Ruhose, Thomsen and Weilage shared the following research:

> *Updating skills and abilities over the life cycle is crucial for workers, firms, and entire economies seeking to prevent human capital depreciation and to remain competitive in a globalised and ever-changing work environment (OECD, 2005, 2013). [I]n industrialised countries, participation in continuing education and training (CET) has become widespread. For example, according to the Survey of Adult Skills (PIAAC, 2015), approximately half of adults aged between 25 and 64 years took part in some CET activity (including open or distance-learning courses, private lessons, organised sessions for on-the-job training, and workshops or seminars – some of which might be of short duration) in OECD countries each year. (OECD, 2017, p. 327) (as quoted and cited in Ruhose et al., 2019, Introduction section)*

This shows that for many countries within the Organisation for Economic Cooperation and Development (OECD), the benefits of engaging adult learners to improve all educational and economic outcomes are recognised. Lifelong learning allows individuals globally, in traditional and non-traditional areas of work, to engage in learning processes beyond narrow 'professional' upskilling that may is not broadly applicable.

Additionally, the promotion of re-entry into the workforce by women who have left for various reasons is an example of innovation and a reimagined idea of professional development. There is a need to discursively resituate learning as central to all areas of work and resituate work as taking place in the domestic sphere as well as anywhere else. The process also makes learning a central aspect across emerging technologies, which is a requirement to address ongoing employment disparities and bridge generational gaps related to technological abilities. These gaps can be seen with ChatGPT, which has been a cause for concern among professors and other academic and administrative personnel, especially in Western institutions (Verma, 2023).

A shift towards people- and planet-centred approaches that involves intergenerational learning, and collaborative partnerships would level out many of the divides that have emerged in the traditional education model. Applying this towards the achievement of SDG targets, diverse modes of partnership and methodologies are necessary to successfully link them, as intended. As such, engaging learning across the life cycle is crucial to addressing literacy, digital and technical divides and gender gaps. In this sense, reciprocity in partnerships across adult learning educational engagements remains key to leveraging the many economic and people benefits and reaching cross-cutting SDG targets by 2030.

STUDENT PERSPECTIVE ON THE IMPLEMENTATION OF SDG 4

Students recognise the crucial role that higher education plays in driving social transformation in a globalised world. It has the potential to offer a foundation for people to become active participants in sustainable development and economic diversification, which ultimately leads to social and economic mobility. Quality education in the Global South is often perceived as a leveller for social and economic mobility and has proved to have higher rates of return than in the Global North. However, limited support and insufficient funding pose significant challenges to higher education ecosystems.

Today, studies of higher education point to the sector playing a major role in the (re)production of inequalities rather than the opposite (Sepúlveda et al., 2022). Students are often told that they live in a time where education has been democratised and that access to knowledge and better opportunities are available to everyone. However, this ideal is not realisable for many students who cannot afford the high fees charged by universities, especially if they want to study in the West. Despite an increase in global literacy rates, inequalities persist and are fuelled by a series of political, social, cultural and economic conditions (Sepúlveda et al., 2022). These persisting inequalities continue to plague higher education systems across the world.

Students in the Global South have varied experiences with the implementation of SDG 4 and how it affects their aspirations and concerns within the higher education ecosystem. According to Pierre Bourdieu, as cited by Sepúlveda et al. (2022), cultural knowledge and educational credentials are assets in the class struggle for advantage and, as such, are a form of cultural capital that play a similar role to economic resources. The distribution of cultural capital in society is as unequal as the distribution of economic capital. Thus, those who have more highly valued cultural capital will have more advantageous economic positions in society.

Similarly, for students in the Global South, the success in higher education systems is largely shaped by how an individual's class background affects their ability to 'play the game' of education in which educational systems are always skewed towards middle-class values and culture. In attending a Western-based higher education institution, most students from the Global South must acquire the tools that enable them to play the game. This is a function which, according to Pierre Bourdieu, will depend largely on their possession of economic, cultural and social capital (Sepúlveda et al., 2022).

This, in turn, has a material impact on how students from the Global South can engage their peers and curriculums. The recognition of learning environments as potential settings for creating and enhancing wellbeing, as well as students' own perceptions of wellbeing in learning environments, is often characterised by students' ability to develop as resilient and engaged citizens (Hammond, 2004). However, equally, students in those learning environments are often exposed to different cultural practices when engaging with wellness issues. It is, therefore, vital for higher education systems to consider the importance of cultivating a holistic understanding of wellbeing in learning environments that not only support the growth and development of students from the Global South engaging within Western cultural contexts but also consider the importance of their wellbeing in relation to their learning experiences. This would increase students' ability to engage with the institution from an empowered position and to adapt to the varied cultural contexts, which opens opportunities for employability.

According to a 2022 report by Higher Education Strategy Associates, titled *World Higher Education: Institutions, Students and Funding*, total enrolments across the world have fallen, in part due to changing demographic factors in Eastern Europe and Russia and due to the decrease in short-cycle enrolments in the USA (Williams & Usher, 2022). Yet, the Global South has seen consistent growth. In 2006, the region had 80 million students, and this almost doubled to 150 million by 2018. However, governments in the Global North increase their funding to shift towards a stable body of students and excess funds are allocated for quality education. In contrast, in the Global South, funds are mostly channelled towards increased capacity and access. While limited financing opportunities are made available to students in the Global South, it has become apparent that resource allocation for students from historically marginalised nations, even within the Global South, is not equitable and access to funds is highly controlled. As a result, some students (mostly from African countries) must seek additional forms of funding for their studies (Usher, 2022).

At a private university in the US northeast, for example, financial support is often available for students in STEM disciplines but difficult to receive for students in the humanities. In addition, various schools in that university allocate their funding to a certain group of students from the Global South, with far more funds allocated directly to their citizens based on need rather than merit. While the intention is admirable, it unfortunately creates a barrier to entry for many students from outside the USA across the higher education system. This calls for governments in the Global South to partner with those schools to deliver on some of the strategic initiatives that are required for educational reform, as encapsulated in SDG 4 targets.

The exchange of cultural knowledge is vital for innovation to take place. Internationalisation and collaboration between universities in the Global South and Global North will allow universities in the ecosystem to expand their horizons and enhance their academic programmes while addressing local challenges and fostering sustainable development.

CONCLUSION

SDG 4 is linked to the other SDGs and its attainment largely depends on strategic partnerships that aim to benefit all. The delivery of this goal calls for the adoption of multifaceted approaches to development and leadership (One Young World, n.d.a). These approaches include strategies for the creation of multisectoral and globally diverse partnerships that recognise the importance of equity in the co-creation of global solutions. The partnerships called for go beyond institution-to-institution partnership and require government and private-sector involvement. Students have voiced their concerns around affordable education not only in their own countries but more so in institutions in the Global North where they wish to study. Also related to this issue is the need for Western institutions to be sensitive to cultural differences and create environments that are nurturing for students to grow and learn.

Recent developments include calls for and attempts to decolonise curriculums. There is an increased demand for higher education, as rising enrolment figures, particularly in the Global South, point to. The main concern is ensuring that, to avoid wasting valuable resources, the systems do not 'mass-produce' graduates who end up unemployed or underemployed. There is also a need for lifelong learning and training graduates who can adapt to changes in the world as well as the resulting shift in industry needs. Creating lifelong learning opportunities makes education more inclusive while supporting development agendas.

REFERENCES

Bennett, N., & Lemoine, G. J. (2014, January–February). *What VUCA really means for you*. Harvard Business Review. https://hbr.org/2014/01/what-vuca-really-means-for-you

Castells, M. (2004). Informationalism, networks, and the network society: A theoretical blueprint. In M. Castells (Ed.), *The network society: A cross-cultural perspective* (pp. 3–45). Edward Elgar.

Chatlani, S. (2018, January 24). *8 global trends impacting higher ed*. Higher Ed Dive. https://www.highereddive.com/news/8-global-trends-impacting-higher-ed/515272/

Chien, C., & Chiteng, F. (2012). New patterns in student mobility in the Southern Africa development community. *Building Regional Higher Education Capacity Through Academic Mobility, 3*(1), 4–21. https://sarua.africa/vol-3-no-1-2011-building-regional-higher-education-capacity-through-academic-mobility/

Clark, C., Cluver, M., & Selling, J. J. (2023). *Higher education's new era*. Deloitte Insights. https://www2.deloitte.com/us/en/insights/industry/public-sector/articles-on-higher-education/higher-education-topics.html

Cloete, N., Maassen, P., Fehnel, R., Moja, T., Gibbon, T., & Perold, H. (Eds.). (2004). *Transformation in higher education: Global pressures and local realities in South Africa*. Kluwer Academic.

Hammond, C. (2004). Impacts of lifelong learning upon emotional resilience, psychological and mental health: Fieldwork Evidence. *Oxford Review of Education, 30*(4), 551–568. http://dx.doi.org/10.1080/0305498042000303008

Higher Ed Dive Team. (2023, December 1). *A look at trends in college consolidation since 2016*. Higher Ed Dive. Retrieved January 29, 2024, from https://www.highereddive.com/news/how-many-colleges-and-universities-have-closed-since-2016/539379/

Hill, K., Hoffman, D., & Rex, T. R. (2005). *The value of higher education: Individual and societal benefits*. Centre for Competitiveness and Prosperity Research. https://core.ac.uk/reader/79586660

Korten, D. C. (1987). Third generation NGO strategies: A key to people-centered development. *World Development, 15*(1), 145–159. https://doi.org/10.1016/0305-750X(87)90153-7

Lane, J., & Murray, T. S. (2018). *Literacy lost: Canada's basic skills shortfall*. Canada West Foundation. https://cwf.ca/wp-content/uploads/2018/12/2018-12-CWF_LiteracyLost_Report_WEB-1.pdf

Microsoft. (2017). *Why Europe's girls aren't studying STEM* [White paper]. Microsoft Philanthropies. https://news.microsoft.com/wp-content/uploads/2017/02/Microsoft_girls_in_STEM_final-Whitepaper.pdf

Ministry of Foreign Affairs of Japan. (1996). *Japan's ODA annual report* [White paper]. Association for Promotion of International Cooperation. https://www.mofa.go.jp/policy/oda/summary/1996/index.html

Moja, T. (2018, November 6–7). *Strategic partnerships as a key driver for Africa's higher education and research system renewal* [Keynote address]. SGCI 2018 Annual Forum, Abidjan, Côte d'Ivoire.

Nicolaides, A., Lim, A., Herr, N., & Barefield, T. (Eds.) (2024). *Reimagining adult education as world building: Creating learning ecologies for transformation*. Routledge.

Noble, S. U. (2018). *Algorithms of oppression: How search engines reinforce racism*. NYU Press.

OECD. (2005). *Promoting adult learning. Education and training policy*. OECD Publishing. https://doi.org/10.1787/9789264010932-en

OECD. (2013). *OECD skills outlook 2013: First results from the survey of adult skills*. OECD Publishing. http://dx.doi.org/10.1787/9789264204256-en

OECD. (2017). *Education at a glance 2017: OECD indicators*. OECD Publishing. http://dx.doi.org/10.1787/eag-2017-en

One Young World. (n.d.). *Lead2030 challenge for SDG 4*. https://www.oneyoungworld.com/lead2030/22-23/challenge-sdg4-deloitte

Ruhose, J., Thomsen, S. L., & Weilage, I. (2019). The benefits of adult learning: Work-related training, social capital, and earnings. *Economics of Education Review*, 72, 166–186. https://doi.org/10.1016/j.econedurev.2019.05.010

Schneider, B., Alexander, J., & Thomas, P. (2023). *Publications output: U.S. trends and international comparisons* (Report no. NSB-2023-33). National Science Board, National Science Foundation. https://ncses.nsf.gov/pubs/nsb202333/

Schofer, E., Ramirez, F. O., & Meyer, J. W. (2020). The societal consequences of higher education. *Sociology of Education*, 94(1), 1–19. https://doi.org/10.1177/0038040720942912

Sepúlveda, D., Mendoza Horvitz, M., Joiko, S., & Ortiz Ruiz, F. (2022). Education and the production of inequalities across the Global South and North. *Journal of Sociology, 58*(3), 273–284. https://doi.org/10.1177/14407833211060059

Silberg, J., & Manyika, J. (2019, June 6). *Notes from the AI frontier: Tackling bias in AI (and in humans)*. McKinsey Global Institute. https://www.mckinsey.com/~/media/mckinsey/featured%20insights/artificial%20intelligence/tackling%20bias%20in%20artificial%20intelligence%20and%20in%20humans/mgi-tackling-bias-in-ai-june-2019.ashx

Sors, T. G., O'Brien, R. C., Scanlon, M. L., Bermel, L. Y., Chikowe, I., Gardner, A., Kiplagat, J., Lieberman, M., Moe, S. M., Morales-Soto, N., Nyandiko, W. M., Plater, D., Rono, B. C., Tierney, W. M., Vreeman, R. C., Wiehe, S. E., Wools-Kaloustian, K., & Litzelman, D. K. (2023). Reciprocal innovation: A new approach to equitable and mutually beneficial global health partnerships. *Global Public Health, 18*(1), 2102202. https://doi.org/10.1080/17441692.2022.2102202

UNDESA. (n.d.). *Youth and intergenerational partnerships* [Fact sheet]. https://www.un.org/esa/socdev/documents/youth/fact-sheets/youth-intergenerational-partnerships.pdf

UNESCO. (n.d.a). *Sustainable development goal 4 (SDG4)*. https://www.unesco.org/sdg4education2030/en/sdg4

UNESCO. (n.d.b). *Target 4.3 – Technical, vocational, tertiary and adult education*. https://gem-report-2017.unesco.org/en/chapter/target-4-3-technical-vocational-tertiary-and-adult-education-2/

UNESCO. (2022, September 20). *Education data release for SDG 4 and other relevant policy indicators*. https://uis.unesco.org/en/news/education-data-release-sdg-4-and-other-relevant-policy-indicators

UNESCO. (2023a, April 20). *What you need to know about higher education*. https://www.unesco.org/en/higher-education/need-know

UNESCO. (2023b, September 7). *UNESCO: Governments must quickly regulate Generative AI in schools*. https://www.unesco.org/en/articles/guidance-generative-ai-education-and-research

United Nations. (n.d.). *Ensure inclusive and equitable quality education and promote lifelong learning opportunities for all*. https://sdgs.un.org/goals/goal4#progress_and_info

United Nations. (2015, September 25). *Transforming our world: The 2030 Agenda for sustainable development.* https://sdgs.un.org/2030agenda

United Nations. (2023, September 20). *The world needs a new model of planet-centred participatory development: UN expert* [Press release]. https://www.ohchr.org/en/press-releases/2023/09/world-needs-new-model-planet-centred-participatory-development-un-expert

Usher, A. (2022, March 15). *The rise and dilemma of the global South.* Higher Education Strategy Associates. https://higheredstrategy.com/the-rise-and-dilemma-of-the-global-south/

Verma, P. (2023, August 13). Professors have a summer assignment: Prevent ChatGPT chaos in the fall. *The Washington Post.* https://www.washingtonpost.com/technology/2023/08/13/ai-chatgpt-chatbots-college-cheating/

Weingarten, E. (2017, November 9). The STEM paradox: Why are Muslim-majority countries producing so many female engineers? *Slate.* https://slate.com/human-interest/2017/11/the-stem-paradox-why-are-muslim-majority-countries-producing-so-many-female-engineers.html

Williams, J., & Usher, A. (2022). *World higher education: Institutions, students and funding.* Higher Education Strategy Associates. Available: https://higheredstrategy.com/world-higher-education-institutions-students-and-funding/

Yarmoshuk, A. N., Cole, D. C., Mwangu, M., Guantai, A. N., & Zarowsky, C. (2020) Reciprocity in international interuniversity global health partnerships. *Higher Education, 79,* 395–414. https://doi.org/10.1007/s10734-019-00416-1

Zavala, M. (2016). Decolonial methodologies in education. In M. A. Peters (Ed.), *Encyclopedia of educational philosophy and theory.* Springer. https://doi.org/10.1007/978-981-287-532-7_498-1

2

EQUAL OPPORTUNITIES IN EDUCATION

Ramola Ramtohul

University of Mauritius, Mauritius

ABSTRACT

The imperative of equality and equal opportunity is a thread that runs through the entire Sustainable Development Goals (SDGs) framework, recognising its ubiquitous nature, its importance as a challenge and the need to address it vigorously. Target 4.3 of SDG 4 requires that by 2030, governments should ensure equal access for all women and men to affordable and quality technical, vocational and tertiary education, including university. The idea of equality, however, goes beyond access. It implicitly extends to equal opportunities to acquire the necessary knowledge, skills and capabilities through educational processes and within educational systems. Moreover, equal opportunities for all remain a key concern for education to be inclusive. Inequality is inherent in the higher education system with wide disparities in the availability and quality of higher education between regions, countries and universities. Limited opportunities for access to quality higher education in many countries are leading to knowledge gaps that have significant consequences for social and economic development. This chapter explores the principal dimensions of inequality in the higher education sector that hinder the attainment of SDG 4. Using a wide-angle lens, the chapter examines the key underlying factors that drive inequality in education, inequality across the education lifecycle and the special characteristics of discrimination. The chapter also explores strategies that can help reduce inequalities in the higher education sector.

Keywords: Disability; gender; higher education; inclusive education; minority groups; race; social class

INTRODUCTION

The imperative of equality and equal opportunity is a thread that runs through the entire SDGs framework. This shows a recognition of its ubiquitous nature, its importance as a challenge and the need to address it vigorously. The focus of SDG 10, for example, is to 'reduce inequality within and among countries', with target 10.3 geared towards ensuring equal opportunities and ending discrimination. This is also a central issue in SDG 4 target 4.3, which specifically requires states to ensure equal access for all women and men to affordable and quality technical vocational education and training, including university education, by 2030.

The idea of equality, however, goes beyond access and implicitly extends to equal opportunities to acquire the necessary knowledge, skills and capabilities through educational processes and within educational systems. Equal opportunities in education should also entail the confluence of and respect for differences among students. This is vital to ensure that the education system provides equal opportunities to all students, but achieving this is a persistent challenge.

Inequality is inherent in the higher education system, with wide disparities in the availability and quality of higher education between regions, countries and even universities. This type of inequality is largely contingent on income and access to resources. Limited opportunities in terms of access to quality higher education in many countries are leading to a 'knowledge gap with serious consequences for social and economic development' (UNESCO, 2015, p. 15). These inequalities translate broadly to disparities in income and social identity and gender representation. In this context, target 4.9 of SDG 4 highlights the need to make adequate funds available to students from developing countries for enrolment in higher education.

This includes funding for vocational training and information and communication technology (ICT), and technical, engineering and scientific programmes, in developed and developing countries by 2030. This is important to mitigate against the impact of knowledge gaps that mostly affect women; ethnic, religious and other minorities and people from low-income backgrounds. As such, without quality higher education, many developing and low-income countries will not be able to progress in a sustainable and inclusive manner (Hoosen et al., 2009, p. 30).

Inclusive education entails the right to education for all, guaranteeing the presence, participation and progress of all students and ensuring equal opportunities (Medina-García et al., 2020). But questions around human rights and equal opportunities remain central to thinking about inclusive education (Amstrong et al., 2016). Target 4.5 of SDG 4 takes the issue further, calling for the elimination of all discrimination in education by 2030. This includes rooting out gender disparities and ensuring equal access to all levels of education and vocational training for vulnerable groups, including persons with disabilities, indigenous populations and children in precarious situations. Inclusive education is, therefore, expected to transform education systems to respond to the diverse needs of students to materialise the right to education with equal opportunities (UNESCO, 2011).

The implementation of policies that promote inclusivity can, however, be problematic within and between educational systems in industrialised as well as less developed countries alike. Whereas effectiveness tends to be more closely related to student management in countries in the Global North, in the Global South, inclusive education is linked with the social and political identities of economic development (Medina-García et al., 2020, p. 4). Violent conflicts and political instability in many African countries have had a devastating impact on universities in these countries. They have led to the destruction of infrastructure, a dearth of academics and censorship of academic freedom (Aina, 2010). An innovative higher education system that contributes to capacity building is, as such, crucial for the achievement of sustainable development and growth in developing countries that suffer from weaker institutional capacity and limited human capital (Salmi & Bassett, 2010, p. 590).

This chapter explores the key dimensions of inequality in the higher education sector that hinder the attainment of SDG 4. Using a wide-angle lens, the chapter examines the key underlying factors that drive inequality in education, inequality across the education lifecycle and the special characteristics of discrimination. The chapter also explores strategies that can help reduce inequalities in the higher education sector.

THE ROLE OF UNIVERSITIES AND CHALLENGES IN THE NEOLIBERAL ERA

Higher education institutions are well placed to contribute to sustainable development, broadly, and the achievement of SDG targets specifically. This can be done through research, knowledge production, skills development and engagement, in the communities, countries and regions where they are situated (Heleta & Bagus, 2021, p. 164). Equal access to higher education is a matter that assumes significance globally. Accordingly, higher education is a strategic tool that contributes to the upward social mobility and reduced socioeconomic inequality.

Access to higher education has also been defined as a driver for democratic socialisation and citizenship (Post et al., 2004). Higher education institutions, particularly universities, primarily hold the responsibility to develop models for global justice and to mobilise a critical mass of academic support. This involves obtaining the support of academics and academic institutions and shaping a culture that supports the attainment of SDG 4. In a globalised and digital era, an increasing number of universities across the world are extending their academic programmes overseas through ICTs, especially the internet, and are developing internationally mixed research themes and creating international curricular initiatives. Teranishi et al. (2015) contend that it is important to ensure that equitable access to higher education remains a key component of the transnational research and policy agenda (p. xi).

Public higher education systems across the world have opened access to university education to a wider range of citizens, providing opportunities that had previously been denied to disadvantaged groups specifically. However, this has not translated to a parallel increase in resources invested in the sector (Ilie & Rose, 2016). The dominant higher education strategy in the West in the 1970s and 1980s was aimed at broadening access to public universities. However, by the turn of the century, the strategic focus shifted to the marketplace, rather than the state, in determining the direction of higher education. This shift was made clear through the rising cost of education (Lazin et al., 2010, p. 1).

As neoliberal education policies are increasingly being implemented, it has become clear that they are key enablers of increased inequality in general. These policies have led to, among other things, increased stratification; rationalised subjects, courses and institutions; reduced diversity; limited innovation; commodification and inferior quality of student learning; wasted resources and the digression of universities from their role as autonomous centres of learning towards being commercial suppliers of educational services (Brown, 2018, p. 40).

Competition for resources and social status has fuelled inequalities in the higher education sector. There have also been reductions in government funding, and a decrease in affirmative action and other programmes that are designed to broaden access to university education (Lazin et al., 2010). Diminished government funding has also meant significant increases in tuition fees, making it more difficult than usual for them to enrol and eventually graduate.

Reduced government funding for higher education has also worsened racial and class inequality. For example, in the USA, rising tuition fees have deterred Black students and those from low-income backgrounds from enrolling at universities (Mitchell et al., 2019). In South Africa, for example, government-subsidised university education (part or in full) has not increased sufficiently to meet the costs associated with higher education. This culminated in the #FeesMustFall student protests in 2015 and 2016, where students demanded free education (Griffiths, 2019). The higher cost of university education risks jeopardising the future of students and that of their communities and localities, as the latter increasingly rely on educated workforces to grow and thrive.

Inequalities in the higher education sector stem from the discriminatory distribution of resources based on prevailing ideologies and philosophies that are not inclusive (Reinders et al., 2021, p. 867). Major challenges in developing countries' higher education sectors include weak public institutions, limited quality education provided by the private sector in terms of private education and/or training, poor infrastructure and facilities, shortage of qualified academics and lack of resources and capacity to meet the demands due to reduced national and international support (Heleta & Bagus, 2021, p. 164).

It has been argued that the expansion of higher education might have contributed to increased economic inequality (Brown, 2018, p. 37). In the UK, for example, students from more privileged backgrounds benefitted the most from the sector's expansion, which, in effect, widened participation gaps between them and students from low-income backgrounds (Blanden & Machin, 2013). Kirp (2010) identifies a few key themes that explain the inequalities that persist in the higher education sector. Ethnic and economic gaps remain strongly anchored in many countries, even with the implementation of policies that promote increased access to higher education. This problem is made apparent by the percentage of students from low-income backgrounds who may not enjoy the benefits of an expanded education system. Expansion in this sense has generated inadvertent negative effects due to policies not being implemented properly, leading to a lack of emphasis on preparing students from low-income backgrounds.

As state subsidies to public universities have been declining, private institutions are seeing an increase in enrolments (Lebeau & Oanda, 2020). Established universities, especially in developed countries, and some in the Global South, have set up satellite campuses in countries in the Global South. While such a policy does expand access to higher education in lower- and middle-income countries, it does not strengthen local higher education capacity and can potentially undermine local initiatives. A key problem with the provision of education by foreign, often Western, universities in countries of the Global South is they do not necessarily serve the best interests and specific needs of host countries and often provide education as consumer product/commodity (Heleta & Bagus, 2021). It has also been found that while private higher education has a strong positive association with overall enrolment in Central and Eastern Europe, as well as core Anglophone countries, there is a weak negative association with access in sub-Saharan Africa (Buckner & Khoramshahi, 2021).

The growing institutional inequality between universities globally and regionally is a key feature in the higher education landscape. Yet, to be able to meet local, regional and global challenges, universities that contribute to development and progress through teaching, research and engagement assume crucial importance to countries (Heleta & Bagus, 2021, p. 167). The institutional status of research universities is reproduced by selective entry and research performance, which feed into each other. In elite universities, for example, high-performing students bring status to the institution, thereby reproducing its exclusivity. These students also receive and benefit from the advantages of institutional brand status as graduates.

The educational mission of universities drives the accumulation of revenue needed to sustain research performance in a competitive market, whereas superior research lifts institutional status with its power to attract top students (Marginson, 2014, p. 4). There is also considerable competition for academic staff among elite universities. Renowned academics are wooed by well-resourced universities across the world, which sometimes offer lavish salaries and generous funding for research and facilities (Kirp, 2010, p. 17). As a result, middle- and low-income countries suffer from a 'brain drain' as their most qualified and productive scholars leave their home universities and countries for 'greener pastures' in the developed world.

The mismanagement and neglect of the higher education sector in much of postcolonial Africa has weakened the continent's universities significantly (Aina, 2010, p. 24). This systematically disadvantages students from underprivileged backgrounds as they are unable to benefit from the knowledge and teaching of high-ranking scholars.

In the post COVID-19 era, which is dominated by digital technology, there is a greater need for internationalisation, equitable partnerships and alliances between universities in different regions. This can help tackle some of the challenges and discrepancies in the quality of education and opportunities. In this sense, the COVID-19 pandemic catalysed the use of digital platforms for teaching and learning to cross geographical boundaries.

The use of such platforms can be enhanced, especially where better resourced universities collaborate with those that are less resourced through partnerships and alliances to offer joint degrees, collaborative research and capacity building for staff and students. One such alliance is the Africa–Europe Clusters of Research Excellence, a collaboration of African and European universities geared towards promoting collaborative research, equity and transformation in higher education, including capacity building for master's and PhD candidates in Africa. The School of Oriental and African Studies at the University of London has also developed a strategy that involves equitable partnerships with universities of the Global South. This is leading to the offering of joint degrees at a lower cost to students.

EXCLUSIONARY FACTORS

The sections below discuss some of the key factors that exclude and/or marginalise students from accessing and benefiting from higher education. Attending to these factors is important to ensure equality and equity in terms of opportunities to access universities and, ultimately, to graduate.

Social Class

Higher education has historically been seen as one of the key drivers of social mobility (Brown, 2018). However, social class has had an ongoing influence on determining which students are able to benefit from university education. Those from underprivileged backgrounds and those who lack financial resources tend to be under-represented and disadvantaged at all levels of higher education and beyond. The total cost of university education includes direct costs such as tuition fees and living costs, study materials and health coverage, as well as indirect costs such as earnings foregone.

Early life experiences, weak cultural capital and learning trajectories are key contributing factors to the marginalisation of students from disadvantaged backgrounds. Whereas a significant proportion of these students may drop out from school before becoming eligible to attend university, the problem of unpreparedness persists among those who are eligible (Herbaut & Geven, 2019). These students tend to experience higher drop-out rates and are less likely to find their way into high paid professions (Crawford et al., 2016). Students from disadvantaged backgrounds also tend to struggle with the challenge of earning enough money to cover their living expenses while studying. Working long hours to supplement income ultimately restricts their capacity to learn and their performance and also limits their focus (Letseka & Pitsoe, 2014). This often means that students either take longer to graduate or, in most cases, drop out completely (Choitz & Reimherr, 2013).

While many universities across the world have financial aid schemes in place, more focused action needs to be adopted to tackle the root causes of marginalisation. Students from disadvantaged backgrounds face a range of barriers to attaining higher education including financial barriers, unpreparedness, lack of information and behavioural as well as cultural barriers (Herbaut & Geven, 2019, p. 3).

Outreach policies are broadly effective in raising access when they include active counselling or simplify the university application process, but not when they only provide general information on higher education. Financial aid in terms of needs-based grants does not systematically raise enrolment rates at university. These grants only lead to improvements when they provide sufficient funds to cover unmet needs and/or include an early commitment during high school (Herbaut & Geven, 2019).

Heleta and Bagus (2021) caution that the acute focus of SDG 4 on sending students from low-income countries to study overseas on scholarships is problematic (p. 165). They contend that there is a greater need to invest in, reinforce and rebuild local universities and deliver quality education to young people, especially in the Global South. As such, concerted investment in upgrading the infrastructure and academic resources of universities of the Global South is important to enhance quality education and greater equality.

Gender

Gender is another determining factor when it comes to accessing higher education in many countries. SGD 5, which focuses on gender equality, aims to achieve gender equality and empower all women, especially girls. Target 5.1 of SDG 5 aims to end all forms of discrimination against women and girls everywhere. Education for women and girls, therefore, remains a central element in the SDG agenda. Patriarchal gender norms have historically privileged boys for university education while marginalising girls. With global legal reforms towards gender equality and equal rights, women and girls have increasingly been able to benefit from university education. In fact, education has major implications for women's status with respect to gender relations throughout society.

Nevertheless, gender remains a barrier to entry into higher education for many girls. In India, for example, young men are on average more likely to gain access to higher education than young women (Ilie & Rose, 2016). The gender gap in higher education there has widened and gender biases in parental expectations have been noted to negatively affect girls (Sánchez & Singh, 2018). In Nepal, education decisions tend to be made by parents and husbands, leading to women being under-represented as students and faculty members (Witenstein & Palmer, 2013). Education for girls remains highly pertinent in all regions, but in the case of developing countries, research has shown that women with higher levels of education tend to marry later, are more likely to use contraceptives, have smaller families and have their first child later than less educated women (Schultz, 1993).

The reproduction of cultural gender norms in higher education institutions significantly affects the labour expectations for girls, with marriage often being a key reason for girls dropping out. In other words, gender-biased norms and stereotypes impact on women's access to higher education as well as their integration into the labour market. They also lead to performance-related issues because women tend to combine their studies with a heavier load of domestic responsibilities than men. Gender-biased socialisation also channels women and girls towards what are considered more feminine fields of study, such as the social sciences and humanities, whereas fields in the 'hard sciences' such as engineering, commerce and medicine are almost entirely reserved for men. This split often places men in key economic areas of activity and women in the opposite, which has bearing on income and economic empowerment. This is despite an increasing number of women pursuing university education.

Apart from women and girls, gender-biased norms and stereotypes also affect sexual minorities, more pertinently students who identify as lesbian, gay, transexual, queer and intersex (LGBTQI). Crane et al. (2020) argue that heterosexism on university campuses leads to hostility and 'micro-aggression' towards LGBTQI students. This limits sexual and gender minority students' social engagement and academic completion. Sexual minority students also tend to be particularly vulnerable to psychological distress (Wolff et al., 2016). These students are also victims of more subtle forms of marginalisation in the higher education setting that are often overlooked, including anti-LGBTQI jokes and social rejection, as well as lack of access to sexual minority role models, limited inclusion of LGBTQI topics in curriculums and insufficient support services (Meyer et al., 2011).

More concerted action needs to be taken by universities to educate students, staff and the wider community on the serious effects of gender-biased norms and stereotypes towards women and girls, as well as towards sexual minorities. Universities need to ensure that gender is mainstreamed across curriculums in all programmes so that graduates are gender-sensitive adults.

There is a need to showcase successful women in 'non-traditional' professions, especially in the fields of science, technology, engineering and mathematics, as role models to encourage and empower girls to enter these fields. Universities also need to have policies in place that protect students and staff from all forms of harassment, especially towards women and sexual minorities. Universities have the knowledge and profound ability to raise awareness on this important issue and can make significant strides towards gender equality and gender equity in society. Training on gender policies and gender sensitivity, as well as capacity building for academic and non-academic staff at universities can also help reduce gender biases in higher education.

Disability

People with disabilities, who are often marginalised at different levels, tend to be underrepresented in the labour force in countries across the world. This is somewhat initiated by barriers to entry to attend higher education institutions for a variety of reasons (Vlachou & Papananou, 2018). Inclusivity, as a strand running through the entire SDG agenda, is imperative for higher education institutions. Veitch et al. (2018) argue that the dropout rate of students with disabilities remains high despite institutional commitments to ensure that these students have adequate access.

The prevailing exclusionary approach, sometimes inadvertently so, requires conformity in terms of physicality and psyche to attain quality education. To counter this, a social justice approach should be adopted to ensure that people with disabilities contribute to and benefit from higher education (Evans et al., 2017).

Developing an inclusive culture requires the promotion of values and attitudes that respect students with disabilities as individuals with agency rather than 'others' or outsiders who have different learning needs and abilities. Accordingly, the structural, organisational, physical and attitudinal aspects of universities should be reconsidered to ensure that students with disabilities have equal and equitable opportunities to benefit from higher education.

Students with disabilities also face barriers to social integration on university campuses (Leake & Stodden, 2014, p. 399). There is a need to ensure that university campus environments are inclusive and welcoming to all minority groups, including students with disabilities. To do this, universities could employ a greater number of academic and support staff with disabilities, for example, and raise awareness on how to accommodate people with special needs on campus. This will require an upgrading of infrastructure to enable accessibility. The availability of support services and awareness workshops can also help disabled staff and students feel more integrated on university campuses.

Race and Ethnic Minority Groups

In some countries, race and ethnic ethnic identities have also significantly impacted on people's attainment of higher education. This problem has been more pronounced in industrialised countries such as the USA and the UK, as well as South Africa in the Global South. In the USA, university enrolment of students of colour has persistently been lower than that of white students. Black American students were also more likely to borrow and accrue higher levels of debt to fund university education (Espinosa et al., 2019). There have been numerous calls to end systemic racism, including in the science, technology, engineering and mathematics fields. This is because policies around diversity have not had any meaningful impact (Barber et al., 2020). Structural racism remains very much present in universities at all levels, from faculty staff to students, in the USA. In the UK, institutional racism is argued to be inherent in universities and students of colour tend to have lower success when compared with white students (Mirza, 2018).

Across the world, students from minority and marginalised groups are more severely impacted by the neoliberal transformation of the higher education sector, given the often existing and entrenched racist institutional practices that are compounded by financial barriers to entry in higher education institutions. In South Africa, Black students often struggle to pay university fees due to their disadvantaged backgrounds (Elliott-Cooper, 2018). As a result, these students tend to face multiple factors of exclusion, including those related to race and class. Pilkington (2018) argues that 'colour-blind government strategies' to broaden participation and promote equal opportunities have little impact on decreasing race inequality (p. 32). Actions need to be more targeted to ensure that students from ethnic minority groups have equal and equitable opportunities to enrol and graduate. Universities also need to promote race equality and ethnic diversity to ensure inclusivity and advancement. Scholarships directed specifically at underrepresented groups can help students who struggle financially, especially where university fees are concerned.

CONCLUSION

This chapter has provided a broad overview of the inequalities that persist in the higher education sector. Through this discussion, the need for concerted action at all levels for education to be inclusive, and for equal opportunities to become a reality, has emerged as a vital component to attain SDG 4. Investment in higher education is fundamental towards fostering more equal societies and maintaining stability and peace (Naidoo, 2011; UNESCO, 2015).

When adequately funded and accessible, higher education can play a crucial role in achieving sustainable development and progress (Heleta & Bagus, 2021). To expand access, there is a need to design financial aid schemes that target needy students. To do so, more resources must be invested into educational institutions that need it the most. Investment in high-quality, affordable and accessible public higher education is crucially important towards attaining SDG 4. Global and regional partnerships between well-resourced and the under-resourced universities, especially those in the Global South, are necessary to ensure equitable access to quality education and to enhance knowledge creation.

Quality education is also critically important for building the capacity that is necessary for development, progress and socioeconomic and environmental sustainability. Low-income countries need to be provided with comprehensive support and assistance to rebuild and strengthen their higher education systems. To ensure equitable access to quality education, it is also important to reduce barriers to skill development and technical and vocational education and training and to provide lifelong learning opportunities to young people and adults. Tertiary education should progressively be made free, in line with existing international agreements.

More concerted attention needs to be given to vulnerable groups, such as people from gender and sexual minorities and people with disabilities and racial and ethnic minorities. This should be done to encourage and facilitate people from these groups to enrol at universities. Higher education institutions should also ensure that the culture on their campuses is inclusive and respects and protects diversity among students.

Despite the considerable challenges they face, universities in the Global South are nonetheless making progress in the way of providing quality education. One example is Kwame Nkrumah University of Science and Technology in Ghana that was ranked first on the Times Higher Education World University Rankings in 2023 for its response to SDG 4, ahead of universities in the Global North. Although there is still a long way to go before quality education becomes a reality, it is not an impossible endeavour.

REFERENCES

Aina, T. A. (2010). Beyond reforms: The politics of higher education transformation in Africa. *African Studies Review*, 53(1), 21–40.

Armstrong, F., Armstrong, D., & Barton, L. (2016). *Inclusive education: Policy, contexts and comparative perspectives*. Routledge.

Barber, P. H., Hayes, T. B., Johnson, T. L., Márquez-Magaña, L., & 10,234 signatories (2020). Systemic racism in higher education. *Science*, 369(6510), 1440–1441. https://kuscholarworks.ku.edu/bitstream/handle/1808/30762/Systemic%20racism%20in%20higher%20education.pdf?sequence=1&isAllowed=y

Blanden, J., & Machin, S. (2013). Educational inequality and the expansion of UK higher education. *Scottish Journal of Political Economy*, 60(5), 578–596.

Brown, R. (2018). Higher education and inequality. *Perspectives: Policy and Practice in Higher Education*, 22(2), 37–43. https://doi.org/10.1080/13603108.2017.1375442

Buckner, E., & Khoramshahi, C. (2021). Does the private sector expand access to higher education? A cross-national analysis, 1999-2017. *International Journal of Educational Development*, 84, 102410. https://doi.org/10.1016/j.ijedudev.2021.102410

Choitz, V., & Reimherr, P. (2013). *Mind the gap: High unmet financial need threatens persistence and completion for low-income community college students*. Center for Law and Social Policy.

Crane, P. R., Swaringen, K. S., Rivas-Koehl, M. M., Foster, A. M., Le, T. L., Weiser, D. A., & Talley, A. E. (2020). Come out, get out: Relations among sexual minority identification, microaggressions, and retention in higher education. *Journal of Interpersonal Violence*, 37(9–10), 8237–8248. https://doi.org/10.1177/08862605209671

Crawford, C., Gregg, P., Macmillan, L., Vignoles, A., & Wyness, G. (2016). Higher education, career opportunities, and intergenerational inequality. *Oxford Review of Economic Policy*, 32(4), 553–575. https://doi.org/10.1093/oxrep/grw030

Elliott-Cooper, A. (2018). '"Free, Decolonised Education" – A lesson from the South African student struggle. In J. Arday & H. S. Mirza (Eds.), *Dismantling race in higher education: Racism, whiteness and decolonising the academy*. Palgrave Macmillan.

Espinosa, L. L., Turk, J. M., Taylor, M., & Chessman, H. M. (2019). *Race and ethnicity in higher education: A status report*. American Council on Education.

Evans, N. J., Broido, E. M., Brown, K. R., & Wilke, A. K. (Eds.). (2017). *Disability in higher education: A social justice approach*. Jossey-Bass.

Griffiths, D. (2019). #FeesMustFall and the decolonised university in South Africa: Tensions and opportunities in a globalising world. *International Journal of Educational Research*, 94, 143–149. https://doi.org/10.1016/j.ijer.2019.01.004

Heleta, S., & Bagus, T. (2021). Sustainable development goals and higher education: Leaving many behind. *Higher Education*, 81, 163–177. https://doi.org/10.1007/s10734-020-00573-8

Herbaut, E., & Geven, K. (2019). What works to reduce inequalities in higher education? A systematic review of the (quasi-)experimental literature on outreach and financial aid. *Research in Social Stratification and Mobility*, 65, 100442. https://doi.org/10.1016/j.rssm.2019.100442

Hoosen, S., Butcher, N., & Njenga, B. (2009). Harmonization of higher education programmes: A strategy for the African Union. *African Integration Review*, *3*(1), 1–36.

Ilie, S., & Rose, P. (2016). Is equal access to higher education in South Asia and sub-Saharan Africa achievable by 2030?. *Higher Education*, *72*(4), 435–455. https://doi.org/10.1007/s10734-016-0039-3

Kirp, D. L. (2010). The earth is flattening: The globalization of higher education and its implications for equal opportunity. In F. Lazin, M. Evans, & N. Jayaram (Eds.), *Higher education and equality of opportunity: Cross-national perspectives*. Lexington Books.

Lazin, F., Evans, M., & Jayaram, N. (2010). Introduction: Higher education and equality of opportunities. In F. Lazin, M. Evans, & N. Jayaram (Eds.), *Higher education and equality of opportunity: Cross-national perspectives*. Lexington Books.

Leake, D. W., & Stodden, R. A. (2014). Higher education and disability: Past and future of underrepresented populations. *Journal of Postsecondary Education and Disability*, *27*(4), 399–408.

Lebeau, Y., & Oanda, I. O. (2020). *Higher education expansion and social inequalities in sub-Saharan Africa: Conceptual and empirical perspectives* [UNRISD working paper, No. 2020-10]. United Nations Research Institute for Social Development (UNRISD).

Letseka, M., & Pitsoe, V. (2014). The challenges and prospects of access to higher education at UNISA. *Studies in Higher Education*, *39*(10), 1942–1954. https://doi.org/10.1080/03075079.2013.823933

Marginson, S. (2014). *Clark Kerr and the Californian model of higher education*. University of California, Berkeley, Center for Studies in Higher Education, Research and Occasional Paper Series: CSHE.12.14. University of California.

Medina-García, M., Doña-Toledo, L., & Higueras-Rodríguez, L. (2020). Equal opportunities in an inclusive and sustainable education system: An exploratory model. *Sustainability*, *12*(4626), 1–20. https://doi.org/10.3390/su12114626

Meyer, I. H., Ouellette, S. C., Haile, R., & McFarlane, T. A. (2011). "We'd be free": Narratives of life without homophobia, racism, or sexism. *Sexuality Research & Social Policy, 8*, 204–214. http://dx.doi.org/10.1007/s13178-011-0063-0

Mirza, H. S. (2018). Racism in higher education: What then, can be done?. In J. Arday & H. S. Mirza (Eds.), *Dismantling race in higher education: Racism, whiteness and decolonising the academy*. Palgrave Macmillan.

Mitchell, M., Leachman, M., & Saenz, M. (2019). *State higher education funding cuts have pushed costs to students, worsened inequality*. Center on Budget and Policy Priorities.

Naidoo, R. (2011). Rethinking development: Education and the new imperialism. In R. Kong, S. Marginson, & R. Naidoo (Eds.), *Handbook on globalization and higher education*. Edward Elgar.

Pilkington, A. (2018). The rise and fall in the salience of race equality in higher education. In J. Arday & H. S. Mirza (Eds.), *Dismantling race in higher education: Racism, whiteness and decolonising the academy*. Palgrave Macmillan.

Post, D., Clipper, L., Enkhbaatar, D., Manning, A., Riley, T., & Zaman, H. (2004). World Bank okays public interest in higher education. *Higher Education, 48*(2), 213–229. https://doi.org/10.1023/b:high.0000034315.98795.c8

Reinders, S., Dekker, M., & Falisse J. B. (2021). Inequalities in higher education in low- and middle-income countries: A scoping review of the literature. *Development Policy Review, 39*, 865–889. https://doi.org/10.1111/dpr.12535

Salmi, J., & Bassett, R. M. (2010). Transforming higher education in developing countries: The role of the World Bank. *International Encyclopaedia of Education, 4*, 590–596.

Sánchez, A., & Singh, A. (2018). Accessing higher education in developing countries: Panel data analysis from India, Peru, and Vietnam. *World Development, 109*, 261–278. https://doi.org/10.1016/j.worlddev.2018.04.015

Schultz, T. P. (1993). Returns to women's education. In E. M. King & M. A. Hill (Eds.), *Women's education in developing countries: Barriers, benefits and policies*. Johns Hopkins University Press.

Teranishi, R. T., Pazich, L. B., Knobel, M., & Allen, W. R. (Eds.). (2015). *Mitigating inequality: Higher education research, policy and practice in an era of massification and stratification*. Emerald Group Publishing Ltd.

United Nations Educational, Scientific and Cultural Organization. (2011). Global education digest. *Comparing education statistics across the world. Secondary education approach*. UNESCO.

United Nations Educational, Scientific and Cultural Organization. (2015). *Education 2030: Incheon declaration and framework for action: Towards inclusive and equitable quality education and lifelong learning for all*. UNESCO.

Veitch, S., Strehlow, K., & Boyd, J. (2018). Supporting university students with socially challenging behaviours through professional development for teaching staff. *Journal of Academic Language and Learning, 12*(1), 156–167. http://journal.aall.org.au/index.php/jall/article/view/526/293

Vlachou, A., & Papananou, I. (2018). Experiences and perspectives of Greek higher education students with disabilities. *Educational Research, 60*(2), 206–221. https://doi.org/10.1080/00131881.2018.1453752

Witenstein, M. A., & Palmer, B. (2013). Inequality of participation in Nepalese higher education: A critical conceptual model of educational barriers. *Asian Education and Development Studies, 2*(2), 162–176. https://doi.org/10.1108/20463161311321439

Wolff, J. R., Himes, H. L., Soares, S. D., & Kwon, E. M. (2016). Sexual minority students in non-affirming religious higher education: Mental health, outness, and identity. *Psychology of Sexual Orientation and Gender Diversity, 3*(2), 201–212. http://dx.doi.org/10.1037/sgd0000162

WEBSITES

African Universities Research Alliance (ARUA) and The Guild of European Research Intensive Universities (The GUILD): https://www.the-guild.eu/news/2023/universities-launch-africa-europe-clusters-of-research-excellence.html

SOAS University of London: https://www.soas.ac.uk/about/news/soas-announces-third-equitable-partnership-university-global-south

The Global Goals – 17 Goals: https://www.globalgoals.org/goals/

Times Higher Education Impact Rankings 2023: Quality Education: https://www.timeshighereducation.com/rankings/impact/2023/quality-education

3

ACHIEVING SDG 4: A CHALLENGE OF EDUCATION JUSTICE

Gerald Wangenge-Ouma[a], Emmanuel Manyasa[b] and Patrick Effiong Ben[c]

[a]*University of Pretoria, South Africa*
[b]*Usawa Agenda, Kenya*
[c]*The University of Manchester, UK*

ABSTRACT

The main point in this chapter is that Sustainable Development Goal (SDG) 4 targets cannot be achieved without education justice, which entails that every child, young person and adult benefit from quality education and lifelong learning. There is no justification for the injustices arising from poor-quality education and exclusion as they exist today. Accordingly, tackling the problem of social, political and economic exclusion that emerges from the education sector, and the limitations they impose on the prospects of some individuals, must be prioritised to expedite the realisation of SDG 4. That entails, among other things, ensuring inclusive and equitable quality education and promoting lifelong learning opportunities for all. Drawing on the nexus between education justice in basic and higher education, this chapter exposes the nature of the challenges that sustain the injustices of educational exclusion and poor-quality education. These include the knock-on effects that injustices in basic education have on higher education, especially for students from marginalised schools. Interventions that seek to advance education justice towards the attainment of SDG 4 are also discussed.

Keywords: Basic education; education justice; education injustice; higher education; quality education; SDG 4

INTRODUCTION

All societies, regardless of their prevailing political dispensations, face the problem of inequality in one form or another (Scanlon, 1996). Inequalities in society are sometimes a product of deep-seated historical structures (e.g. the legacy of apartheid in South Africa and ethnic and regional marginalisation in Kenya). They must be addressed if a society is to make meaningful progress without leaving anyone behind. Poverty; socioeconomic exclusion; racial, ethnic and gender marginalisation and other forms of inequality are all examples of what needs to be addressed to advance equitable human progress and the realisation of all 17 SDGs.

A casual stroll through our streets and institutions today reveals an abundance of injustices in all forms. Particularly worrisome are injustices in the education sector, which threaten not just our ability to achieve SDG outcomes, but the future of our societies and planet. As Chimakonam (2019) states: '[A] badly educated citizenry is the first enemy of the state' (p. 181). This means that the lack of access to quality education for all citizens has the potential to breed poorly educated, sometimes miseducated, citizens who endanger society. As such, access to quality and equitable education for all becomes a matter of justice. Broadly, quality education serves as an important, if not the most important, leveller in modern society. Achieving the outcomes of SDG 4, which broadly aims to ensure inclusive and equitable quality education and promote lifelong learning opportunities for all, is an essential part of tackling these inequalities and realising global social justice. Yet, equal access to quality education remains out of reach for many of those who need it most (Azevedo et al., 2021; Gust et al., 2024; UNICEF & AUC, 2021).

This chapter frames the challenge of achieving SDG 4 outcomes as a challenge of education justice. The underlying aim of SDG 4 is to expand opportunities across all phases in the education system. In this sense, education justice is a focal area in SDG 4. The goal's targeted outcomes reinforce this focus as they seek to ensure, among other things, access to quality education across all phases of education. In essence, this means that education is equally distributed to all children, young people and adults across demographics, including people with disabilities, indigenous peoples and those from vulnerable groups. Unterhalter (2019) describes SDG 4 as a 'victory for proponents of a vision of quality education that was orientated to ... equalities' (p. 40). Focusing on the higher education phase, this chapter examines the advancement of SDG 4 through the lens of education justice.

Education justice is necessary for any modern society to attain meaningful development. Its prevalence guarantees an adequate quality of life for its people. However, a lack of education justice may be framed as a problem of human development (Sen, 1999). This translates to a struggle for 'a fully adequate quality of life and for minimal justice' among socially and culturally excluded, economically disadvantaged and politically marginalised people (Nussbaum, 2011, p. 16). In this sense, education justice, which guarantees the 'human minimum' of a decent standard of living for the world's poor and excluded, becomes a catalyst for global justice and collective human development (Oruka, 1997).

This chapter examines the idea of education justice within the broader movement of equality. As we argue that education justice is a precursor for achieving the SDG 4 outcomes, we highlight challenges that sustain the injustices of educational exclusion and poor-quality education, and some interventions that have been implemented to speed up change, advance education justice and, ultimately, attain SDG 4.

WHAT IS EDUCATION JUSTICE?

Education justice could be understood as an expansive concept with divergent and contextually driven understandings. It often has similar objectives to goals that are set for achieving academic inclusion and economic redistribution, among other opportunities, for those in marginalised groups. To Nieuwenhuis (2010), the notion of educational equality, or equity, is based on the idea that 'the state must guarantee a set of liberties, implying that [everyone] shall have the right to equally good education', irrespective of their social, economic, political, cultural or family background (p. 273). To Cazden (2012), education justice includes 'ensuring access … to an intellectually rich curriculum for all students, especially those whose families and communities have been denied that access in the past' (p. 182). This is based on the common understanding that good quality education is part of the answer to poverty alleviation (Connell, 1991).

For Tan (2020), social justice is generally conceived to be concerned with the provision of social arrangements that allow everyone to participate fully and equally in the affairs of society. To guarantee equally good education and its associated liberties to every child, young person and adult, the state must ensure, among other things, that more resources are allocated and be involved in the process of dismantling the barriers that prevent marginalised people from participating equally with others as full members of society (Rawls, 1971; Sen, 1992; Tawney, 1964). The latter makes equity central to the notion of education justice. In unequal societies, education justice has become a necessity for the same reasons we care about gender equality/justice, economic justice and climate justice, among others.

Conceptually, the notion of education justice suggests two distinct but interrelated concepts, education and justice. Education is a fundamental human right. Access to it enables individuals to realise their full potential (capabilities) and take advantage of opportunities that offer development and expanded economic activities. This approach offers students the flexibility to develop their unique capabilities and, as such, reflects their freedom to lead their choice of life to achieve their basic functioning. This is in line with the capabilities approach of Sen (1983, 1985, 1992) and Nussbaum (1997, 2011).

Education justice may also be understood from the perspective of its conceptual opposite, education injustice. This is because claims about the need for social, political and economic justice, in any form, are mostly discussed in relation to injustices, marginalisation and disadvantages, which are often the outcome of social exclusion (Daniels et al., 2022). In this analysis, we conceive of education justice as a situation where the provision of and participation in quality education prevails. That is, when guarantees for every child, young person and adult to benefit from quality education, including lifelong learning, are in place. However, accessibility is not the only condition for good quality education. The availability of resources that are required by the different groups of learners (e.g. those with disabilities) should also be ensured, as well as other enablers of quality and equitable access.

The idea of education justice is suggestive of, among other things, education as a tool for ensuring full and meaningful participation in economic, social, political and cultural life. It is a pathway for socioeconomic mobility, and a tool for providing substantive opportunities for all people to develop the capabilities needed to lead a life of value and to participate fully in the social, economic and political life of one's community. These ideas present quality education as one of the 'primary goods' – to use Rawls's (1971) term – that every rational person is not just presumed to want but should be entitled to as a member of the human community. The elimination of injustice and the achievement of SDG 4 in this sense become what philosophers such as Scanlon (1996) call 'a political objective of the first importance' (p. 1). Consequently, this is a constitutional responsibility of all states and a moral imperative in general.

While for many years since the declaration of education as a human right in 1948, education justice has focused mainly on basic education, the right to higher education continues to receive increased attention. This has been driven by, among other things, the widespread acknowledgement of the value of higher education in socioeconomic advancement towards a common good for society (Sabzalieva et al., 2022).

Significant strides have been made in advancing access to higher education. However, many young people, especially in sub-Saharan Africa, remain excluded (Darvas et al., 2017; Lebeau & Oanda, 2020; Mtawa et al., in press). Examining higher education in relation to SDG 4, particularly from a social justice perspective, highlights persisting challenges. For example, inequitable access based on geography and socioeconomic backgrounds, and the changes that need to be made to address the different needs of students from diverse backgrounds.

This section has provided a conceptualisation of the idea of education justice within the broader context of social justice. It provides useful background for framing the subsequent discussion on challenges that sustain education injustice and efforts that are aimed at advancing education justice and the attainment of SDG 4.

WHAT IS EDUCATION INJUSTICE?

An analysis of education injustice in higher education would be incomplete without highlighting its existence in basic education. Broadly, students who are excluded from basic education would automatically be excluded from higher education. Similarly, students who receive poor-quality basic education have a lower chance of gaining access to higher education, and those who make it are often not adequately prepared for higher education. In other words, achieving justice in higher education would be a challenge if injustice persists in basic education. This section exposes various challenges that sustain education injustice in basic education as a lead-in for highlighting education injustice in higher education.

In 2021, UNICEF and the African Union Commission (AUC) reported that access to basic education in Africa has improved significantly. The proportion of children of primary school age who are not in school has reduced by more than 50%, from 35% in 2000 to 17% in 2019. Similarly, the proportion of children of upper secondary school age who are not in school decreased from 63% to 53% over the past two decades. However, significant challenges remain. The report estimates that, in 2019, there were 105 million children of primary and secondary school age who were not enrolled in school. In the same year, on average, one in three children in a cohort does not complete primary school (UNICEF & AUC, 2021). This excluded children who do not stand a chance of participating in higher education.

One problem is the number of unqualified teachers in primary and secondary schools in many poor and developing countries. For example, according to Adeyeye (2020), as much as 38% of primary school teachers and 24% of junior secondary school teachers in Nigeria are unqualified. Recruiting unqualified teachers to address teacher shortages in rural schools, as a way of achieving education for all, in countries like Zimbabwe has been reported to result in 'lower quality education and student achievements' (Mukeredzi, 2016, p. 1).

Many studies have highlighted the phenomenon of 'exclusion from learning'. An assessment of learning in Kenya's basic education system that was conducted by the Uwezo Kenya (2021) and Usawa Agenda (2022) revealed low learning levels, especially among learners in rural areas, and an inequitable distribution of teachers and other educational resources. Similarly, the Progress in International Reading Literacy Study, which assesses reading comprehension and monitors trends and indicators of growth in reading literacy, has consistently shown gaps in the reading achievement of grade 4 learners in South Africa. Results of a study conducted in 2021 by the International Association for the Evaluation of Educational Achievement, which were released in 2023, show that 81% of grade 4 pupils in South Africa could not read for meaning.

While significant strides have been made to advance equity in education and gender equality, intractable challenges persist. These challenges arise from, among other things, structural factors such as the inequitable distribution of educational and other resources, as well as gender norms and cultural beliefs, which skew the parity of participation, especially for girls. An understanding of the intersectionality of gender with other drivers of inequality is critical in advancing gender equality in education. As such, to address barriers to gender equity and equality in education effectively, a gender transformative approach must concern itself with the various interacting drivers of gender inequality. These include cultural norms; beliefs and practices; discriminatory gender stereotypes; poverty; safety and disability.

While enrolments in higher education have increased significantly, entrenched inequalities that mirror those in basic education persist. Learners who are subjected to poor basic education have a limited chance of participating and succeeding in higher education. Generally, higher education in sub-Saharan Africa is only accessible to a small elite. The proportion of each cohort that gets access to higher education yearly ranges from 9% to 10% in the region. As described by Darvas et al. (2017), this is a consequence of deeply entrenched patterns of inequitable access to higher education, indicating that the sector has failed to address the challenges brought on by the inequalities it is meant to dismantle. As the authors further observe, 'patterns of access to tertiary education in sub-Saharan Africa have generally reinforced and reproduced social inequality rather than eroding its pernicious social and economic effects' (p. xv).

The COVID-19 pandemic highlighted some of the systemic challenges that hinder the realisation of both equitable access and outcomes in higher education in Africa. A study by Mtawa et al. (in press) concluded that while the adoption of digital technologies and pedagogies during the pandemic was well-intentioned, it increased inequality of access. This is because it disproportionately benefited universities and students who had adequate access to information and communication technology (ICT) and connectivity, and the knowledge to use them, at the institutional and household levels. Of equal importance to access is the question of quality. Wangenge-Ouma and Langa (2014) have highlighted the phenomenon of 'exclusion from within' in higher education institutions, where students gain access to university but are excluded from a meaningful relationship with knowledge. In this sense, they acquire credentials but do not learn sufficiently.

Financial resources are among the most critical assets that universities depend on to enhance access and offer high-quality education. This makes it essential for universities to sustain their financial health. However, all university systems across the world are facing financial challenges in varying degrees. The COVID-19 pandemic exposed widespread differences and inequalities in terms of institutional resource capacities to manage the crisis and its costs. For this reason, many higher education institutions were unable to embody changes and put strategies in place that dealt with providing grants, reducing tuition fees and providing digital learning resources. These measures were commonly adopted in upper-income countries to ensure access for students (Mtawa et al., in press).

Although universities across the world experienced funding-related challenges during COVID-19, these were deeper in sub-Saharan Africa, given the region's history of underfunding. In Kenya, for instance, university funding for the 2021/2022 financial year was cut by 9%. Kenya's public universities were allocated KES 99.9 billion compared to KES 109.3 billion in the previous financial year. Audit reports of public universities in Kenya show that many of them are financially insolvent. In South Africa, funding for universities was cut by R7.7 billion in 2021/2022 (National Treasury, 2021). The cuts also affected student financial aid, which had implications for student access and participation.

Some of the responses by universities to funding cuts have had negative implications for accessibility. In 2021, the University of Nairobi increased tuition and other fees significantly to address funding challenges. The university's enrolment data for 2022 show a decline in enrolments by 7,795 students (from 55,488 students in 2020/2021 to 47,693 in 2021/2022). This decrease in enrolment is attributed to the university's significant increase in tuition and other fees (Kenya National Bureau of Statistics, 2022).

Another manifestation of education injustice takes the form of epistemic oppression, defined by Dotson (2014) as the 'persistent and unwarranted infringement on the ability to utilise persuasively shared epistemic resources that hinder one's contributions to knowledge production' (p. 116). This hindrance according to Dotson often takes the form of an 'unwarranted infringement on the epistemic agency of knowers' (p. 115), or the deliberate epistemic exclusion of a particular group of knowers, for example, women in patriarchal societies, minority groups in multicultural societies and indigenous populations in settler-colonial societies.

Broadly, epistemic oppression may be understood to encapsulate the unjust exercise of authority in the conception, production, structuring, justification and dissemination of knowledge and ways of knowing by one group – with dominant powers and advantages – over another. In other words, it is a form of oppression related to knowledge and knowing subjects. To Fricker (1999), this form of oppression is best captured when society is organised in a way that accords unfair advantages to the powerful, who then use these advantages to 'structure' people's perception of the social world to their advantage (p. 191).

The epistemic oppression of women is a form of gender-based injustice that systematically excludes women from knowledge-making practices. It involves the structuring of epistemology in a way that silences women's perspectives in the production, legitimisation and dissemination of knowledge and ways of knowing. This could happen when: an unfair advantage (or more epistemic credibility) is given to the ideas and opinions of men over women in the production and justification of knowledge; the overall value of women's education and the quality of their intellectual contributions is called into question and there are unfriendly academic environments that are insensitive to the epistemic needs of women in the knowledge production process (Mkhize, 2022; Muhanguzi, 2019). Overall, epistemic oppression manifests in ways such as curriculums that perpetuate harmful stereotypes against women and marginalised communities, pedagogical approaches that engender passive learning, language and communication patterns that limit the participation of learners in the classroom and assessment practices that prioritise a narrow set of knowledge and skills (Omodan, 2023).

As injustices in basic education have a direct bearing on injustices in higher education, interventions to enhance education justice in higher education are necessary, among other reasons, to address the challenges in basic education. The right to higher education cannot be achieved when millions of children are excluded from basic education or are subjected to poor-quality basic education.

ADVANCING SDG 4 THROUGH EDUCATION JUSTICE INTERVENTIONS

Several studies have been carried out on education justice across the world. Most of these have focused on basic education, perhaps because of its foundational role. However, such studies have important lessons for higher education. In East Asia, China specifically, Tan (2020) offers an interesting empirical perspective of social justice education with Chinese characteristics. According to Tan, Shanghai's Municipal Education Commission developed a social justice education model that attends primarily to 'educational equity between schools rather than between students' (pp. 1,393–1,398). What this means is that the policy prioritises the inclusion of weak schools, rather than students, in the high-quality index.

This shift in focus offers an insightful perspective on redistributing resources in a way that reduces the gap not just between individuals, but between groups and societies. Perhaps, the most important lesson from this approach is that when inclusion is directed at individuals instead of groups, achieving community economic mobility becomes difficult. This is due to the limited compound effect of individual progress. Inequalities between educational institutions are equally pronounced within higher education systems. In South Africa, for example, the higher education landscape is broadly characterised by two types of universities: historically advantaged institutions and historically disadvantaged institutions (HDIs). The former are relatively well-resourced and are located mainly in major urban areas. During apartheid, these universities were for white students only. HDIs, however, were reserved for Black population groups and are still generally under-resourced and located in marginalised areas.

The South African government has implemented various initiatives to address the plight of HDIs to ensure that they provide quality education to the many poor students who attend these institutions. Initiatives include the HDI Development Grant, which was renamed the Sibusiso Bengu Development Programme in 2022. Objectives of the grant include strengthening institutional management and governance structures; improving infrastructure for learning and teaching, research, student housing and ICT; enabling effective staff recruitment, retention and progression and enhancing student life and success. Overall, the grant seeks to address the inequalities that negatively impact the development and sustainability of HDIs.

Cuba's example offers one of the most renowned success stories of a state-sponsored education justice programme. In 2008, the

Latin American country channeled as much as 14% of its GDP to education investments, substantially higher than most other countries across the world. This government policy was motivated by the common understanding that 'only good-quality, empowering education could conquer Cuba's acute poverty, ignorance and underdevelopment' (Kronenberg, 2015).

Inadequate infrastructure is often cited as one of the problems that developing countries face in their attempt to provide quality education to all. However, due to the rigorous combination of formal and informal learning, inadequate facilities in Cuba do not seem to impinge on the educational outcomes of Cuban students. In fact, according to Bearman (2020), 'Cuba's students in the worst state schools test similarly on most academic tests as some of the best private schools elsewhere in Latin America'. This is attributed to 'an emphasis on teacher quality, receiving education from a young age, consistent teacher training and assistance, and a strong national curriculum, which is lacking in many other states'. Based on Cuba's example, it can be deduced that the advancement of education justice on a large scale, where equity and excellence are pursued, is an achievable goal. Initiatives in this respect include affirmative action, engagement with communities and innovation in teaching and learning.

Kenya offers a good example of affirmative action in higher education. The country's university placement policy provides for affirmative action in terms of gender, people with disabilities and those from marginalised/minority communities. As part of the policy, university entry requirements are lowered by two points for women where the entry requirement is higher than C+ (C+ is the minimum overall grade required for university admission), and specific programme requirements are lowered for the benefit of the underrepresented groups. As Fig. 3.1 illustrates, this has resulted in the gender gap being narrowed in technical and vocational education and training (TVET) colleges and public higher education institutions, from 50% before 2000 to 10% in 2000 (Muraguri, 2020).

Gender representation has also improved in several programmes. For example, the percentage of women in the health

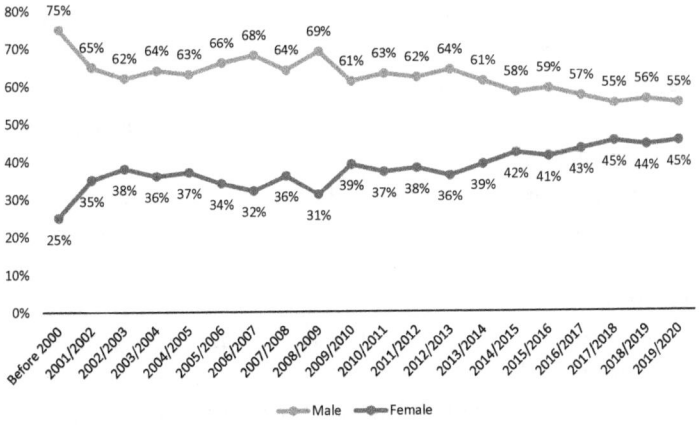

Fig. 3.1. Gender Representation in TVET and University Placement in Kenya.
Source: Muraguri (2020).

sciences (medicine, nursing and pharmacy) has increased from 34% in 2014/2015 to 41% in 2019/2020 and in engineering from 18% to 24% over the same period (Muraguri, 2020).

Community engagement programmes constitute a critical pathway through which universities and other higher education institutions support the enrolment of students from especially marginalised communities. The University of Pretoria (UP) in South Africa offers a good example. To ensure that a greater number of students from marginalised communities can participate in higher education, some of the university's programmes are aimed at building stronger connections with schools that serve these communities.

Through its JuniorTukkie programme, UP carries out initiatives that seek to enhance the academic preparation of students in grades 9–12 and encourage their attendance at UP. The university's Tuks Leadership and Individual Programme (dubbed TULIP), which was founded in 2016, is a student-led initiative whereby UP students voluntarily tutor promising high school learners in marginalised areas. The initiative has five components: leadership development and mentorship, academic support and tutoring, financial education and bursary support, human development and application support. An equally important initiative is the university's Pre-University Academy (PUA), which was established in 2018, which aims to broaden university access to students from marginalised communities in STEM (science, engineering, technology and mathematics) programmes by addressing the high school-university gap prior to entry into tertiary study. Within the suite of PUA programmes (post-secondary school readiness and awareness, teacher professional development, and engendering scientific literacy) is a Saturday school programme that presents seven courses (mathematics, physical science, natural science, creative writing, language and literacy skills, computer literacy and examination preparation) for learners in grades 8–12, which is aimed at complementing their schoolwork. PUA aims to eventually reach more than 30,000 beneficiaries, including school learners, in-service teachers and adults in the community that do not have formal education.

The COVID-19 pandemic made online learning a necessity. The closure of universities and the consequent inability to continue with face-to-face teaching and learning led to the adoption of large-scale online teaching and learning. As such, the pandemic offered universities the opportunity to rethink new digital, online and pedagogical possibilities. Blended learning provides opportunities for universities to address some of the limitations of the residential educational model. The various blended learning models provide multiple possibilities for innovation. For example, the flex model, where most instruction takes place online with contact sessions as needed, is ideal for students who can only study on a part-time basis, with contact sessions being organised in blocks (Wangenge-Ouma & Kupe, 2020). The flexibility provided by blended learning makes it possible for universities to broaden access to diverse student groups.

Online and blended learning are also important enablers for lifelong learning, reskilling and upskilling. Various studies have emphasised the need for this in the context of the rapid changes in the skills landscape (Azhar, 2021; Smith & Browne, 2021; Wangenge-Ouma, 2022). This requires a shift in the delivery of education towards the provision of flexible lifelong learning opportunities. The aim is to enable people to continuously improve their knowledge, acquire new skills, enhance their working possibilities and improve their overall quality of life.

Many African universities offer various opportunities for lifelong learning through, among other things, evening and weekend programmes, massive open online courses (MOOCs), e-learning and short courses/capacity-building programmes (mainly provided by business schools, campus companies and, increasingly, private companies) and web-based learning resources on platforms such as Udemy. However, the development of MOOCs and web-based learning in Africa is in the nascent stage. This is mainly due to lack of access to requisite technological infrastructure and facilities and inadequate internet connectivity (Wangenge-Ouma, 2022; Wangenge-Ouma & Kupe, 2020; Zeleza & Okanda, 2021). Nevertheless, sustained adoption, expansion and investment in these approaches hold immense promise for reducing education inequalities and ensuring the attainment of inclusive and equitable quality education opportunities for all, from primary to higher education.

CONCLUSION

In this chapter, we have demonstrated that SDG 4 cannot be attained without education justice. As quality education is a human right, there is no justification for the education injustices (exclusion and poor-quality education) that exist today. For this reason, tackling the problem of social, political and economic exclusion perpetuated by regimes of injustice that arise in the education sector must be prioritised to expedite the attainment of SDG 4, which targets inclusive and equitable quality education and the promotion of lifelong learning opportunities for all.

Addressing the injustices that characterise our education systems has policy and other implications. Improving quality would entail, among other measures, increased state investments in balancing the resource inequity that exists between schools and the underfunding that institutions of higher learning face. Teacher training must be prioritised to improve the quality of learning that students receive, no matter the location of their educational institutions. Measures must be put in place to ensure that marginalised and underrepresented groups are not left behind. This will ensure that underrepresented groups, especially in the higher education sector, have a platform to mobilise for economic and general human development. Policies must be designed to be responsive to the needs of individual communities to maximise outcomes as they affect specific groups.

ACKNOWLEDGMENTS

This chapter is derived from a larger study on education justice (equitable access to quality education: toward an education justice agenda) commissioned by Usawa Agenda.

REFERENCES

Adeyeye, P. (2020, August 14). *A review of the basic education situation in Nigeria*. Dataphyte. Retrieved September 29, 2023, from https://www.dataphyte.com/latest-reports/special-report/a-review-of-the-basic-education-situation-in-nigeria/

Azevedo, J. P., Goldemberg, D., Montoya, S., Nayar, R., Rogers, H., Saavedra, J., & Stacy, B. W. (2021). *Will every child be able to read by 2030? Defining learning poverty and mapping the dimensions of the challenge*. The World Bank.

Azhar, A. (2021). *The exponential age: How accelerating technology is transforming business, politics and society*. Diversion Books.

Bearman, T. (2020, Monday, January 20). Education in Cuba: Social protection for human capital development. *socialprotection.org*. Retrieved September 30, 2023, from https://socialprotection.org/discover/blog/education-cuba-social-protection-human-capital-development

Cazden, C. B. (2012). A framework for social justice in education. *International Journal of Educational Psychology*, *1*(3), 178–198.

Chimakonam, J. O. (2019). *Ezumezu: A system of logic for African philosophy and studies*. Springer.

Connell, R. W. (1991). The workforce of reform: Teachers in the disadvantaged schools programme. *Australian Journal of Education*, *35*(3), 229–245.

Dotson, K. (2014). Conceptualizing epistemic oppression. *Social Epistemology, 28*(2), 115–138.

Fricker, M. (1999). Epistemic oppression and epistemic privilege. *Canadian Journal of Philosophy, 29*, 191–210.

Daniels, H., Porter, J., & Thompson, I. (2022, June). What counts as evidence in the understanding of school exclusion in England? *Frontiers in Education, 7*, 929912.

Darvas, P., Gao, S., Shen, Y., & Bawany, B. (2017). *Sharing higher education's promise beyond the few in sub-Saharan Africa*. World Bank Publications.

Gust, S., Hanushek, E. A., & Woessmann, L. (2024). Global universal basic skills: Current deficits and implications for world development. *Journal of Development Economics, 166*, 103205. Retrieved March 10, 2024, from https://doi.org/10.1016/j.jdeveco.2023.103205

Kenya National Bureau of Statistics (KNBS). (2022). *Economic survey 2022*. KNBS.

Kronenberg, C. (2015). *Why Cuba is an education success story and what it can teach Africa*. The Conversation Africa.

Lebeau, Y., & Oanda, I. O. (2020). *Higher education expansion and social inequalities in Sub-Saharan Africa: Conceptual and empirical perspectives (No. 2020-10)*. United Nations Research Institute for Social Development (UNRISD) Working Paper.

Mkhize, Z. (2022). 'They are just women, what do they know?': The lived experiences of African women doctoral students in the mathematics discipline in South African universities. *Transformation in Higher Education, 7*, 218.

Mtawa, N., Munene, I. I., Fongwa, S., Kibona, B., & Wangenge-Ouma, G. (in press). COVID-19 and access to higher education: Achieving social justice or entrenching inequalities? *Journal of Higher Education in Africa, 21*(2).

Muhanguzi, F. K. (2019). Women and girls' education in Africa. In O. Yacob-Haliso & T. Falola (Eds.), *The Palgrave handbook of African women's studies* (pp. 1–18). Palgrave Macmillan.

Mukeredzi, T. G. (2016). The nature of professional learning needs of rural secondary school teachers: Voices of professionally unqualified teachers in rural Zimbabwe. *SAGE Open*, *6*(2), 2158244016643142.

Muraguri, J. (2020, February 17–18). Women and higher education: Gender trends in higher education in Kenya (enrolment and fields of study), and options to promote women participation in higher education. Presentation at the Regional Knowledge Sharing Forum, Nairobi, Kenya.

National Treasury. (2021). *Budget review 2021*. National Treasury.

Nieuwenhuis, J. (2010). Social justice in education revisited. *Education Inquiry*, *1*(4), 269–287.

Nussbaum, M. C. (2011). *Creating capabilities: The human development approach*. Harvard University Press.

Omodan, B. I. (2023). Unveiling epistemic injustice in education: A critical analysis of alternative approaches. *Social Sciences & Humanities Open*, *8*(1), 100699.

Oruka, H. O. (1997). *Practical philosophy: In search of an ethical minimum*. East African Publishers.

Rawls, J. (1971). *A theory of justice*. Harvard University Press.

Sabzalieva, E., Gallegos, D., Yerovi Verano, C. A., Chacón, E., Mutize, T., Morales, D., & Cuadros, J. A. (2022). *The right to higher education: A social justice perspective*. UNESCO.

Scanlon, T. M. (1996, February 22). *The diversity of objections to inequality*. The Lindley Lecture. A Lecture Delivered at the University of Kansas.

Sen, A. (1983). Poor, relatively speaking. *Oxford Economic Papers*, *35*(2), 153–169.

Sen, A. (1985). A sociological approach to the measurement of poverty: A reply to Professor Peter Townsend. *Oxford Economic Papers*, *37*(4), 669–676.

Sen, A. (1995). *Inequality reexamined*. Harvard University Press.

Sen, A. (1999). *Development as freedom*. Oxford University Press.

Smith, B., & Browne, C. A. (2021). *Tools and weapons: The promise and the peril of the digital age*. Penguin.

Tan, C. (2020). Social justice education with Chinese characteristics: An example from Shanghai. *British Educational Research Journal, 46*(6), 1391–1405.

Tawney, R. H. (1964). *Equality*. Unwin Books.

UNICEF & AUC. (2021). *Transforming education in Africa. An evidence-based overview and recommendations for long-term improvements*. A report by UNICEF and African Union Commission.

Unterhalter, E. (2019). The many meanings of quality education: Politics of targets and indicators in SDG 4. *Global Policy, 10*(1), 39–51.

Usawa Agenda. (2022). *Are our secondary schools inequitable by design? Usawa 1st secondary school survey report*. Usawa Agenda.

Uwezo. (2021). *Are all our children learning? Uwezo 7th learning assessment report*. Usawa Agenda.

Wangenge-Ouma, G. (2022). Towards post-coronial futures: COVID:19, rapid digital transformation and university responsiveness. *CODESRIA Bulletin, 12*, 48–56.

Wangenge-Ouma, G., & Kupe, T. (2020). *Uncertain times: Reimagining universities for new, sustainable futures*. Universities South Africa working paper. https://www.usaf.ac.za/wp-content/uploads/2020/09/Uncertain-Times-Paper.pdf

Wangenge-Ouma, G., & Langa, P. V. (2014). *Good access to poor courses won't create real learning*. SciDev.net-Enterprise.

Zeleza, P. T., & Okanda, M. P. (2021). Enhancing the digital transformation of African universities: Covid-19 as accelerator. *Journal of Higher Education in Africa, 19*(1), 1–28.

4

BUILDING CAPABILITY FOR IMPACT: THE MASTER'S IN DEVELOPMENT PRACTICE AT THE UNIVERSITY OF PRETORIA

Samantha Castle[a], Willem Fourie[b] and Dawie Bornman[a]

[a]*University of Pretoria, South Africa*
[b]*Stellenbosch University, South Africa*

ABSTRACT

To effectively address the grand challenges facing humanity, as highlighted in the Sustainable Development Goals (SDGs), society needs to harness talents, realise human potential and build capabilities in people and systems to navigate the associated complexities.

In contributing to SDG 4, universities play a critical role in building impactful capabilities at the undergraduate and postgraduate levels, as well as through their core functions of teaching, learning, research and public engagement. 'Impact' in this context refers to meeting the needs of diverse students and those of local, regional and global communities. In a changing world with changing societal expectations, the pursuit of relevance is also likely to them more competitive and attractive to students.

The Global Association of Master's in Development Practice (MDP) provides an important avenue for illustrating how universities can contribute to achieving SDG 4. This is hinged primarily on building young professionals' capacity to address the challenges articulated in the 2030 Agenda for Sustainable Development.

In this chapter, the development of an MDP degree programme at the University of Pretoria (UP) – within the ambit of its membership to the Global Association of MDP – is used as a case study to illustrate how this explicitly multidisciplinary programme can support the development of leadership capabilities that are needed to achieve the SDGs. The chapter includes theoretical perspectives as well reflections from a student and a supervisor who participated in the programme.

Keywords: Multidisciplinary education; SDG 4; Sustainable Development Goals; sustainability; tertiary education; transdisciplinary education

INTRODUCTION: DEVELOPMENTAL CHALLENGES IN A COMPLEX WORLD

Globally, there is a growing demand for education that equips students with capabilities to deal with the challenges posed by intensified local and global complexities. A significant global concern is centred on environmental sustainability. Recent findings from Copernicus Climate Change Service, for example, revealed that, in 2023, the hottest November ever was recorded worldwide, with an average surface air temperature of 14.22°C. This was 0.85°C higher than the 1991–2020 average for that month and 0.32°C above the temperature of the previously warmest November in 2020 (Copernicus, Climate Change Services, 2023). In addition, a scientific and regulatory agency based in Washington, DC, reported that in May 2022, carbon dioxide levels reached an unprecedented peak in the northern hemisphere (National Oceanic and Atmospheric Administration, 2023).

The escalation of global temperatures, attributed to the emission of greenhouse gases (Mikhaylov et al., 2020), is acknowledged as a primary factor behind widespread catastrophic events such as floods, persistent drought, heatwaves, wildfires, storms and other natural disasters. Consequently, scientists continue to issue alerts about increasing global temperature and the potentially disastrous outcomes, emphasising the critical need to restrict global warming to 1.5°C and limit greenhouse gas emissions. As such, investment in alternative, renewable energy has become urgent.

Substantial social challenges also have adverse effects on the general wellbeing of populations. These include regional conflicts, food security, the availability of clean water and sanitation, poverty, migration patterns, education and health, among others. For example, the consequences of the Russia–Ukraine war have significantly affected the production and export of wheat. This conflict could result in as many as 1.7 billion people experiencing hunger and 276 million people facing severe food insecurity. The ensuing food and energy shortages as well as high inflation have had a ripple effect, causing numerous other countries to face similar issues, leading to ongoing social unrest (Lin et al., 2023).

Globally, the challenges associated with migration – within and outside of home countries – due to conflict persist (Lerpold et al., 2023). However, the estimated number of displaced individuals due to natural disasters surpasses that of refugees fleeing from conflicts. According to the World Bank's Groundswell report, natural disasters linked to climate change might compel approximately 216 million people to migrate by 2050 (Clement et al., 2021). Access to clean water and sanitation is also an ongoing concern. In 2022, it was estimated that 25% of people lacked safely managed drinking water in their homes and about 70% of people in Africa lacked safely managed sanitation services (UNICEF, 2023).

The SDGs were adopted in 2015 by global leaders as a universal call for action 'to end poverty, protect the planet and ensure that all people enjoy peace and prosperity by 2030' (Courtois, 2019). The 17 SDGs and their 169 targets cover interrelated components of sustainable development whether economic, societal or environmental (Ramutsindela & Mickler, 2020). The adoption of the SDGs is an acknowledgement of global challenges and a framework for responding to them. Given the intractable nature of challenges related to sustainability, it is apparent that the UN's Sustainable Development Agenda is of critical importance (Pedersen, 2018).

The knowledge and human capabilities needed to enable the achievement of the SDGs are crucial for their actualisation. As such, universities play an important role in leading the way towards equipping students and professionals with the skills to actively engage with, assess and resolve intricate sustainable challenges.

AN APPROACH TO REFOCUSING UNIVERSITY EDUCATION

The need to refocus university education to respond to the challenges of an increasingly complex world – especially as it relates to sustainable development – was recognised as far back as the 1970s (Bianchi, 2020, p. 2). Since then, there has been a consensus that developing sustainability skills is to effectively address challenges and adapt to ways of living that align with the wellbeing of our planet (Bianchi, 2020, p. 2). However, the absence of a widely accepted and comprehensive competency framework for sustainability had resulted in various interpretations of what constituted knowledge, skills, attitudes and values that are essential for sustainability (Bianchi, 2020, p. 2).

In 2007, the MacArthur Foundation supported the establishment of the International Commission on Education for Sustainable Development Practice at The Earth Institute, which is part of the Columbia Climate School. The commission was mandated to identify 'the core cross-disciplinary educational needs to support problem-solving in the realm of sustainable development' (The Earth Institute at Columbia University and the John D. and Catherine T. MacArthur Foundation, 2008, p. 2).

Considering severe global sustainability challenges, the report specifically identified 'the lack of cross-disciplinary knowledge and skills within the field of sustainable development' (The Earth Institute at Columbia University and the John D. and Catherine T. MacArthur Foundation, 2008, p. 4) as a central challenge.

Their analysis of postgraduate programmes related to sustainable development across the world found that 'most academic degrees relevant to sustainable development ... tend toward academic specialisation within a particular discipline', with 'few opportunities for systematic, cross-disciplinary education or management training' (The Earth Institute at Columbia University and the John D. and Catherine T. MacArthur Foundation, 2008, p. 15). This is illustrated in Fig. 4.1.

In response to this challenge, the commission advocated at a high level for a renewed emphasis on the development of 'generalist' development practitioners. These are people who understand 'the complex interactions among fields and can coordinate and implement effectively by drawing from the insights offered by subject-specific specialists' (The Earth Institute at Columbia University and the John D. and Catherine T. MacArthur Foundation, 2008, p. 14). More specifically, this practitioner should operate at the intersection of four 'spheres' – health sciences, natural sciences, social sciences and management.

A more recent report published in 2020 by the Joint Research Centre (JRC), the European Commission's science and knowledge service, resonates with much of the commission's report. It highlights 'the need to develop a more encompassing system to identify and update the necessary sustainability (instead of green) competencies critical to perform sustainability-related jobs and other jobs in a sustainable manner' (Bianchi, 2020, p. 51). This served

Scan of Current Degree Programs		Health Sciences	Natural Sciences	Social Sciences	Management	"Hands-on Skills"
	Master's of Public Administration	○	○	●	◐	○
	Master's of Development Studies	◐	○	●	○	○
○ low coverage	Master's of Sustainable Development	○	●	◐	○	◐
◐ some coverage	Master's of Business and Administration	○	○	◐	●	◐
● more coverage	Master's of Public Health	●	○	◐	◐	◐
	Medical Doctor (MD)	●	◐	○	○	●

Fig. 4.1. Coverage of Development Knowledge Area.

Source: The Earth Institute and the MacArthur Foundation, 2008, p. 16 © John D. and Catherine T. MacArthur Foundation – used with permission.

as another acknowledgement of the need for broader and cross-disciplinary competencies.

The JRC report also highlights that, based on insights derived from sustainability education, it is recommended and feasible to integrate sustainability competencies into any occupation (Bianchi, 2020, p. 52); and that essential skills, as described in the report as 'key competences', should be linked to roles that are specifically associated with sustainability (Bianchi, 2020, p. 52). In doing so, a case was made for 'the development of sustainability as a transversal key competence to develop and nurture, through lifelong learning, the necessary knowledge, skills, attitudes and values for a sustainable society' (Bianchi, 2020, p. 51).

The International Commission on Education for Sustainable Development Practice concluded the report with four recommendations. The first centred on establishing the 'core competencies of the sustainable development practitioner' (The Earth Institute at Columbia University and the John D. and Catherine T. MacArthur Foundation, 2008, p. 19). In this context, the commission recommended the inclusion of theory and practice from health sciences (e.g. health and epidemiology and population sciences), natural sciences and engineering (e.g. agriculture, energy, environment, water and climate sciences), social sciences (e.g. economics, education and politics) and management (e.g. budget planning, financial management, communications and project management).

The commission's second recommendation proposed the establishment of a Master's in Development Practice (MDP) degree programme. According to the commission, these programmes (The Earth Institute at Columbia University and the John D. and Catherine T. MacArthur Foundation, 2008, p. 24) should provide education for development practitioners to integrate health sciences, natural sciences and engineering, social sciences and management. Importantly, the commission recommended that the curriculum included 'field training' with two separate assignments lasting a total of six months. This would entail work with other entities to offer 'a holistic "clinical" training experience' (The Earth Institute at Columbia University and the John D. and Catherine T. MacArthur Foundation, 2008, p. 7).

The third recommendation focuses on the need for sustainable development professionals to have continued access to professional development. The commission's fourth recommendation was to establish an MDP secretariat and international advisory board.

More difficult than identifying the relatively well-known gaps in postgraduate university education, as identified in the commission's report, was the question of operationalising these four recommendations. To this end, the commission ambitiously proposed the establishment of a global network of MDP degree programmes (The Earth Institute at Columbia University and the John D. and Catherine T. MacArthur Foundation, 2008, p. 24). Included in the conceptualisation of this network of master's degrees is an internship or field practical to ensure that acquired knowledge is applied.

The approach of a generalist development practitioner, as mentioned in the commission's report, entails cultivating the 'key competences' emphasised in the JRC report. These key competencies are put in place to empower individuals to address intricate challenges and create opportunities that promote sustainability (Bianchi, 2020, p. 51).

In the framework linking pedagogical approaches to sustainable development competencies, Lozano et al. (2017) identifies several key skills. These include, among others, 'systems and anticipatory thinking, interdisciplinary collaboration, responsibility and ethics, critical analysis, interpersonal relations, collaboration, change of perspective, communication and media usage, strategic action, personal involvement, assessment and evaluation, and tolerance for ambiguity and uncertainty' (Bianchi, 2020, p. 27).

Since the commission's report was published, the goal of establishing a global network of MDP programmes has borne fruit. At the time of writing, 37 institutions in 26 countries were members of the Global Association of MDP. Many of these institutions participate in the annual Global Classroom event, a 'web-based, graduate-level course that fosters cross-disciplinary collaboration' (Global Classroom, 2023).

LOCALISING THE MDP PROGRAMME

At UP, the need to establish a multidisciplinary master's degree for educating generalist development practitioners initially started without knowledge of the work of the International Commission on Education for Sustainable Development Practice.

In 2012, a group of academics participated in conversations on UP's contribution to research and teaching on Africa's development. Agreement was reached on five points: UP needs to develop a stronger and more explicit institution-wide focus on issues related to the development of Africa; a stronger focus on issues related to Africa's development can enhance its relevance and role in the pursuit of social justice in Africa; UP is ideally positioned to produce research and teaching with an impact on the development of Africa and it needs to grow in its understanding of Africa's developmental challenges.

It was also agreed that a task team with a dual mandate should be convened. It should, firstly, investigate and make recommendations on a multi-faculty MDP programme and, secondly, investigate and initiate a platform for lectures aimed at the broader university community on issues of relevance to development.

In pursuit of the tasks related to the establishment of a multi-faculty MDP programme, a steering committee was convened. Their tasks included: the initial conceptualisation of key aspects related to the introduction of the degree, including a proposal of the structure and an outline of the contents; issues related to its administration, financial implications, its unique features and the added value of the introduction of such a programme and the potential implications of such a programme for research at UP on themes related to development.

The steering committee's conceptual work was the starting point for the proposal of a master's programme with three features:

- It should be African in that it equips candidates with African theory, exposes them to African best practices and instils leadership capacities that are rooted in African experiences.

- It should be multidisciplinary. Candidates will be allowed to specialise in specific policymaking areas, including health, education, tax, peace and security, governance and rural and urban development.

- The degree should be integrative in that it seeks to expose candidates to several disciplines while equipping them with the knowledge, skills, experience and leadership capabilities needed to implement transformative development policies.

As the steering committee's work progressed, there were significant changes in the regional and global development landscape. The implementation of the African Union's Agenda 2063 and its seven aspirations commenced in 2015. Agenda 2063 synthesises the lessons learnt from previous attempts at defining Africa's development agenda and is formulated in response to the uneven development progress in Africa. The implementation of the SDGs, ratified in September 2015, also started. The significant convergence between the SDGs and Agenda 2063 made it possible for the planned multidisciplinary master's degree to incorporate elements from both development agendas.

The focus of the master's subsequently also changed to include a more explicit focus on the achievement of the SDGs, as reflected in the refined competence areas of the programme below:

- *Theoretical competence*: Candidates should understand the theory of sustainable development, SDGs, core SDG disciplines and leadership.

- *Multidisciplinary competence*: Candidates should be able to engage sustainable development challenges and solutions in more than one sector by harnessing multiple academic disciplines' strengths and expertise.

- *Critical competence*: Candidates should gain the competence to respond critically and constructively to the role of business, government and civil society in responding to the SDGs.

- *Leadership competence*: Candidates should gain the competence to reflect on and implement requisite leadership theory, practice, behaviour and values to implement the SDGs.

- *Practical competence*: Candidates should acquire the ability to develop actionable multisectoral responses to the SDGs.

As the finalisation process for the content of the master's degree began, UP became aware of the Global Association of MDP and the practical guidance it provided in designing a programme aimed at developing generalist development practitioners. Accordingly, the guidelines were integrated into UP's approach and the programme would contain an explicit focus on the four broad disciplines.

Its social sciences module includes content from the fields of education, economics, taxation and human rights (covering SDGs 1, 4, 8, 9, 10 and 17). The health sciences module uses SDG 3 as its point of reference and introduces participants to the determinants of health, health systems strengthening and health policy in developing contexts. The module on natural sciences focuses on the challenge of ensuring inclusive and sustainable development with content on climate change, food security and natural resource management. This module responds particularly to SDGs 2, 8 and 13. The leadership module explores the leadership capabilities needed to achieve all SDGs. Emphasis is placed on responsible leadership and relational leadership theories. These theories are contrasted with neo-charismatic and trait-based approaches to leadership.

Guidance from the Global Association of MDP, and the recommendations on which its work is built, also came to be reflected in other ways in UP's programme. The outcome of the programme, for example, is to enable participants 'to understand the complexity of sustainable development challenges, as expressed by the SDGs' and to enable them 'to design multidisciplinary solutions to such challenges' (University of Pretoria, 2024, p. 4).

This programme-level outcome reflects the Global Association's emphasis on integrative and practice-oriented training. This is also reflected in the UP programme's three sub-outcomes (University of Pretoria, 2024, p. 4). Firstly, candidates will be enabled to 'identify, document and interpret a complex sustainable development challenge'. They will, secondly, be guided to 'understand foundational theory in social sciences, health sciences and natural sciences and will be able to integrate foundational theory into multidisciplinary responses to the sustainable development challenges'. Lastly, candidates will be enabled to 'understand foundational leadership theory and will be able to develop an appropriate leadership approach to implementing responses to sustainable development challenges'.

While resonating strongly with the intention behind the establishment of the Global Association of MDP, the approach followed by UP also reveals differences. The most significant difference is that the theoretical component on management emanating from the commission's report focuses chiefly on the leadership capabilities needed to achieve complex agendas such as the SDGs. This is, at least in part, because UP's programme is hosted and presented by a research institute that focuses on the topic of leadership.

A second difference has to do with how the programme is presented. Whereas the assumption in many of the other MDP programmes is that candidates should be present in person at the host university, the UP programme explicitly adopted a hybrid approach where theory lessons are done mostly virtually and solidified through group work and peer mentorship in person. Candidates are on campus only for three contact weeks per year, and these focus on expert engagement, peer exchange, integration and application. Practical group assignments that students receive during their second and third contact weeks entail integrating and applying the theory acquired virtually. These group assignments are typically aimed at developing approaches to addressing a contemporary development challenge. They explicitly require students to integrate insights from multiple disciplines.

The third and possibly most significant difference between the MDP programme offered by UP and the guidelines offered by the Global Association on MDP is how the former handles field training. The rationale for dealing with this element differently starts with the students who are interested in completing the programme at UP. Most interest comes from professionals already in full-time employment, making it financially and practically challenging – if not impossible – to participate in a field training programme away from work. This is why UP opted to use the MDP to enable participants to reflect on development-related initiatives within their workplaces as field training programmes.

Practically, this means that each candidate is expected to identify and analyse an initiative in their workplace that covers more than one of the SDGs' targets as a case study. As such, their guiding research questions should focus on leadership capabilities that enable the delivery of multiple SDGs towards setting up a development-relevant project in their immediate environment.

PARTICIPANT REFLECTIONS

Student Reflection

Fostering development has always remained a central focus throughout my personal and professional journey. This commitment inspired me to organise youth programmes and ignited my passion for social entrepreneurship. I went on to establish a foundation to respond to education and social-related challenges in poor communities in South Africa. However, recognising the complex mesh of societal issues and their interconnectedness, I realised the need to deepen my understanding. Thus, I decided to pursue an MDP, aspiring to deepen my knowledge and refine my approach to sustainable solutions.

Key lessons from the MDP programme:

(a) Sustainable development practice cannot be done in isolation. Through the programme's theoretical framework, I acquired insights and was able to connect the interrelated and intricate nature associated with the SDGs. I soon realised that attempting to address each goal in isolation would be too simplistic. Instead, I recognised the importance of adopting a nuanced approach that would allow for the appreciation and facilitation between environmental, social, economic and governance challenges. This sharpened my ability to ask critical and more holistic questions in examining sustainable challenges.

(b) Collaboration and interdisciplinary dialogues enrich our understanding of complex issues. Having the privilege to participate in classes alongside peers from diverse cultural and professional backgrounds facilitated robust debates and dialogue on complex matters. Through group assignments and team projects, I appreciated a variety of perspectives and approaches to develop solutions. The MDP programme is firmly rooted in the principle of collaboration, which enhanced my

understanding and value of addressing challenges through a multidisciplinary lens.
(c) Practical experience enhances skills and insights. The MDP programme used practical research projects to facilitate learning and sharing of real-life experiences and challenges. Through fieldwork and data analysis, I was able to strengthen my research and analytical skills while bridging theoretical concepts. However, more importantly, through observation and asking questions, I was able to learn valuable lessons on the pivotal role of leadership in fostering collaboration, which is vital for sustainable transformation.
(d) Urgency of action towards sustainable transformation. The sense of urgency to address social and environmental challenges became evident to me during my time in the MDP programme. Engaging with the different case studies, gaining first-hand knowledge of the consequences of sustainable challenges through the literature and research, underscored the urgent need for action. For example, confronting sobering statistics regarding environmental issues such as climate change and associated greenhouse gas emissions, I developed a deeper appreciation for my personal responsibility and dedication to fostering the transition towards a more sustainable environment.

The MDP programme has been a transformative experience for me. It has sharpened my academic abilities and boosted my confidence in addressing complex challenges. Serving as an eye-opener, the programme has encouraged and empowered me to venture further into this field of work. After the MDP, I went on to successfully complete a PhD. The MDP was integral in my academic pursuits. For that, I am truly grateful.

Supervisor Reflection

(a) Comparison with other master's degree programmes

As the MDP is structured in an integrative way, it has various elements that are drawn from other master's degree programmes.

These include the Master's in Philosophy (MPhil) degree, the Master's in Business Administration (MBA) degree and the Master's in Commerce (MCom) degree. The main difference between an MPhil degree and the MDP is that the former is focused purely on research. In many cases, during MPhil studies, there is minimal contact between supervisor and student. Often, students are assigned topics unrelated to their interests within their field of study. This is evident when topics are assigned to students along their supervisors' research focus or field of interest, which is impractical. For an MPhil, students have the option to study either full-time or part-time, and the programme normally comprises either one or two years of study. The student must have a specific undergraduate, honours or postgraduate diploma in a certain field.

On the other hand, a large majority of individuals worldwide who venture into postgraduate studies at the master's level will focus on completing an MBA programme. This type of degree programme is more focused on a broad overview of all areas within the business landscape and requires students to gain a holistic perspective of the business environment instead of focusing on a specific field. Management training is at the heart of any MBA curriculum, with a focus on leadership, planning, business strategy, organisational behaviour and the 'human' aspect of running a large or small business.

In some cases, aspects such as responsibilities and corporate accountability of businesses within their communities are addressed, but the holistic view is more focused on core business skills across areas like marketing, finance and accounting while developing soft skills and leadership skills. Student who falls outside of the management or business field are in some cases required to first complete a graduate management admission test to establish their level of understanding before commencing with the MBA programme. Normally, an MBA degree is presented either full-time or part-time over one or two years, respectively.

In comparison with an MDP programme, an MCom degree programme contains more face-to-face contact on a regular basis (e.g. every month, three days are set aside for seminars). Small assignments are used as assessments that do not necessarily contribute to the overall result but can rather be viewed as 'opportunities' to test whether understanding and interpretations of theory interpreted correctly. An MCom degree could comprise various modules that do not necessarily form a holistic result.

The degree usually has eight modules and a dissertation and is completed over two years. Although there are elements of practical application through some of the assignments, in general, the assessment is more focused on theory and research. A student can only study for an MCom degree if they have an undergraduate, honours or postgraduate diploma in commerce. Studies are focused on subjects related to commerce, accounting, business administration, management and economics. An MCom degree is a research-based programme that is designed to expand intellectual interests by fusing research skills and expertise. It is aimed at developing a student's ability to reflect critically on theory and its application in practice by accurately framing problems, asking focused questions and formulating appropriate strategies for investigating them. However, these questions do not always solve the problems that are identified. Rather, they serve a starting point for discussion on where further investigation needs to take place.

By considering the various master's degree programmes, it is clear that the MDP programme is focused on integrative and practice-oriented knowledge building. Assignments are smaller deliverables that contribute to the final deliverable. As such, the final deliverable is broken down into critical assessments, ensuring that there is constant dialogue between students and their research mentors or supervisors. This enables research mentors or supervisors to assist students in improving their understanding (whether to clarify certain concepts or constructs, or to advise on the correct synthesis of theory with practice).

This reaffirms to the student that the seminars or peer-to-peer learning (through group work) taking place is in line with what their research mentor is expecting of them, as well as how these concepts and constructs are aligned with the vision of their work environments. As the MDP programme is presented through a one-year hybrid approach, it also allows flexibility to students who work in fields where travel is required.

(b) The learning experience and witnessing students' growth in real time

As a research mentor or supervisor, it is clear that students experience an increase in understanding, knowledge building and application during the MDP programme. As all students in the programme are professionals who are already in full-time employment, they are encouraged to reflect on development-relevant initiatives within their workplaces to incorporate the practical application of the MDP programme. Each student is, therefore, expected to identify and analyse an initiative in their work environment that covers more than one of the SDGs' targets as a case study. Upon first consultation with their research mentor or supervisor, most students are unsure of where to start.

As the seminars commence and students interact with each other, their ability to identify initiatives becomes clearer and an element of peer-to-peer learning and consolidation of thoughts and ideas takes place. Students grow in confidence and become more comfortable interacting with like-minded individuals from different work environments. They learn how certain aspects discussed are addressed differently in other work environments and that there is not necessarily only one solution. Students also begin to consult with their research mentors or supervisors prepared with questions or discussion points that they need assistance with. This makes the journey fruitful not only for the students but also for the research mentors or supervisors, as knowledge is not just being disseminated but also shared and synthesised towards finding sustainable solutions.

(c) Relevance of content and topics addressed

The MDP programme's seminars are presented by thought leaders in industry and academia. They aid students to think in an integrative, future-orientated manner through focusing on what can be done in the present to ensure that certain mistakes of the past do not reoccur in the future, or that potential risks identified can be addressed before they possibly become crises. This is all done while thinking about how the programme can support the development of leadership capabilities that are needed to achieve the targets set out in the SDGs and Agenda 2063. The inclusion of the internship or field training practical assessment in the MDP programme helps ensure that the acquired knowledge is applied in practice. In turn, each student's capabilities are enhanced to navigate within their respective working environments while being mindful of sustainability and social challenges.

CONCLUDING REMARKS

In this chapter, we discussed how universities can contribute to the achievement of the 2030 Agenda for Sustainable Development by focusing on SDG 4. The way in which UP developed, customised and delivered the MDP degree programme was used as a case study.

This chapter has shown how – in pursuit of the SDGs and recognising their interconnected nature – it is possible for higher education institutions to pursue a 'middle way'. This is expressed in various ways. Firstly, the chapter dealt with the possibilities of developing a postgraduate programme that is positioned between specialisation in a discipline and an overly generalist approach. It also highlighted how it is possible to position a programme in the middle of the continuum with theory at the one end and practice at the other. Thirdly, we illustrated how a programme that takes guidance from global good practice can be developed for adaptation to local realities. This means incorporating African perspectives on development, rethinking how experiences in the field are dealt with and developing a context-specific thematic focus.

REFERENCES

Bianchi, G. (2020). *Sustainability competences. A systematic literature review*. Publications Office of the European Union.

Clement, V., Rigaud, K., De Sherbinin, A., Jones, B., Adamo, S., Schewe, J., Sadiq, N., & Shabahat, E. (2021). *Groundswell part 2: Acting on internal climate migration*. World Bank. Retrieved March 26, 2024, from http://hdl.handle.net/10986/36248. Licence: CC BY 3.0 IGO.

Copernicus, Climate Change Services (2023). *Copernicus: November 2023 – Remarkable year continues, with warmest boreal autumn.*

2023 will be the warmest year on record. Retrieved February 20, 2024, from https://climate.copernicus.eu/copernicus-november-2023-remarkable-year-continues-warmest-boreal-autumn-2023-will-be-warmest-year#:~:text=November%202023%20was%20the%20warmest,previous%20warmest%20November%2C%20in%202020

Courtois, S. (2019). *The integration of SDGs through intra-sector collaboration: The case of the chemical sector SDG roadmap*. Louvain School of Management, Université catholique de Louvain.

Global Classroom (2023). *Welcome 2023 global classroom students*. Retrieved January 4, 2024, from https://wordpress.lehigh.edu/globalclassroom/2017/08/02/hello-world/

Lerpold, L., Sjöberg, Ö., & Wennberg, K. (2023). *Migration, integration, and the pandemic. Migration and integration in a post-pandemic world: Socioeconomic opportunities and challenges*. Springer International Publishing.

Lin, F., Li, X., Jia, N., Feng, F., Huang, H., Huang, J., Fan, S., Ciais, P., & Song, X. (2023). The impact of Russia-Ukraine conflict on global food security. *Global Food Security*, 36, 100661.

Lozano, R., Merrill, M. Y., Sammalisto, K., Ceulemans, K., & Lozano, F. J. (2017). Connecting competences and pedagogical approaches for sustainable development in higher education: A literature review and framework proposal. *Sustainability*, 9(10), 1889.

Mikhaylov, A., Moiseev, N., Aleshin, K., & Burkhardt, T. (2020). Global climate change and greenhouse effect. *Entrepreneurship and Sustainability Issues*, 7(4), 2897.

National Oceanic and Atmospheric Administration. (2023). *Broken record: Atmospheric carbon dioxide levels jump again: Annual increase in keeling curve peak is one of the largest on record*. Retrieved February 20, 2024, from https://www.noaa.gov/news-release/broken-record-atmospheric-carbon-dioxide-levels-jump-again#:~:text=Carbon%20dioxide%20levels%20measured%20at,of%20California%20San%20Diego%20announced

Pedersen, C. S. (2018). The UN Sustainable Development Goals (SDGs) are a great gift to business!. *Procedia CIRP*, 69, 21–24. https://doi.org/10.1016/j.procir.2018.01.003

Ramutsindela, M. & Mickler, D. (Eds.). (2020). *Africa and the Sustainable Development Goals*. Springer International Publishing.

The Earth Institute at Columbia University and the John D. and Catherine T. MacArthur Foundation (2008). *International commission on education for sustainable development practice: Final report*. Retrieved January 4, 2024, from http://mdpglobal.org/files/2021/11/Final20Report-202008-1.pdf

UNICEF (2023). *Progress on household drinking water, sanitation and hygiene 2000–2022: Special focus on gender*. Retrieved March 26, 2024, from https://data.unicef.org/resources/jmp-report-2023/

University of Pretoria. (2024). *Master's in development practice: 2024 programme guide*. Unpublished.

5

BROADENING ENGAGEMENT AND SOCIETAL RESPONSIVENESS

Jeffrey Grabill[a], Simone Buitendijk[b], Manuel Barcia[a] and Sonia Kumar[a]

[a]*University of Leeds, UK*
[b]*University of Salford, UK*

ABSTRACT

Perhaps the most important question universities need to ask themselves is how they can increase their efforts to meaningfully contribute to resolving the major societal issues of today. Universities are probably the only institutions that, when working together, can truly have a large and sustained influence on the global challenges we face. With that in mind, the fundamental question for universities that we try to answer in this chapter is: How can we ensure and increase our relevance in a way that is ethically and socially responsible? Our metaphor for working through this question is to argue that a university must 'think differently'. We argue in favour of what we consider a pragmatic approach to engagement. To illustrate this approach, the University of Leeds' approach to broaden its engagement and social responsibility both regionally and globally is used as an example. Ultimately, universities that are engaged and socially responsive must strategically redefine excellence towards more generosity and collaboration. Excellence is impossible without social impact and the deep collaborations necessary to deliver it.

Keywords: Civic university; engagement; transformational approaches; knowledge equity; outreach; social responsiveness

INTRODUCTION

Perhaps the most important question universities need to ask themselves is how they can increase their efforts to meaningfully contribute to resolving the major societal issues of today. In many ways, societal impact is the core mission of universities, whether it is achieved through research carried out in close collaboration with societal partners, or through training and educating generations of societally engaged citizens and leaders. Most universities, whether research or teaching focused, will claim they are driven by the positive impact they want to create locally, nationally and sometimes even globally. Yet, in practice, societal impact is often not foregrounded as a strategic goal.

Universities are probably the only institutions that, when working together, can truly have a broad and sustained influence on the global challenges we face. In many ways, they embody the fundamental pillars of the Sustainable Development Goals (SDGs), which centre on people, planet, prosperity, peace and partnerships. Over the last few decades, however, many universities, especially those considered to be in the global top 100 or 200, have learnt to think in terms of competition and global rankings. As such, they have turned inward, not outward. Striving for rankings can produce real value for those institutions (e.g. international student interest), but most universities fall outside that elite rank.

Furthermore, competition and the concomitant university rankings are still largely defined by research outputs such as publications. If competition is such a prominent part of the university culture, and if core behaviours are driven primarily by research outputs that provide individuals and institutions with a competitive advantage, societal engagement and responsiveness will not be primary strategic drivers. Excellence in societal engagement is still poorly defined, difficult to measure and not integrally part of the system of ranking and defining university status and worth. These issues need to be addressed to ensure that incentives are aligned with behaviours that will produce societal impact at scale.

If universities want to play a unique role in making a major difference in the global population's ability to meet the SDGs, they must become more collaborative, less focused on their own narrowly defined success and more willing to share their knowledge and educational capabilities. This will require a concerted, long-term approach, as well as a global mindset, even for smaller, more locally focused higher education institutions. With that in mind, the fundamental question for universities in this chapter centres on whether we can ensure and increase their relevance in a way that is ethically and socially responsible.

As always, the 'how' question is the most challenging. Given the histories, values and infrastructure of universities that were often designed in differently, how could they adjust themselves to be engaged and responsive to societal challenges in a responsible, useful and collaborative way? In this sense, universities must 'think differently'.

The notion that an institution 'thinks' and that it can think in other ways is important. Ideas matter because they, along with values, drive behaviour. If we want universities to behave differently, they need to be animated by new ideas and associated values. In this chapter, we argue for an idea that we consider a pragmatic approach to engagement. We illustrate this idea through an example of how the University of Leeds is thinking and behaving in novel ways that are designed to broaden engagement and societal responsibility, regionally and globally.

UNIVERSITIES AND THE SDGs

The United Nation's recognition that education is a fundamental driver for realising human development goals was slow to develop. However, it has reached a point where education is considered central to sustainable development. In 1961, during the General Assembly's 16th session, a resolution was reached to develop a programme for international economic cooperation. This heralded the beginning of the 1st Development Decade. Such a push, however, had no clear reference to quality education anywhere within its text. Only agenda item (d) vaguely referred to it, suggesting the need for accelerating the elimination of illiteracy along with hunger and disease. Not surprisingly, little progress was made throughout the 1960s. During the General Assembly's 25th session in 1970, the lack of progress made during the previous decade was brought to the fore.

This meeting resulted in a general agreement that declared the decade starting in 1971 as the 2nd Development Decade. This time, the need for access to quality education was noted for the first time in a key UN document. Agenda item 18, for example, highlighted the need to improve educational facilities as other goals were pursued (United Nations General Assembly, 1970). There is a specific demand made here that all children of primary school age should be given access to education. The same agenda stipulated that nations should strive for an improvement in educational quality at all levels to reduce illiteracy, as well as create educational programmes around development needs. Ultimately, this new document called for a commitment from all nations to establish and expand scientific and technological institutions to support such educational and development aspirations.

In December 1979, the UN took a crucial step forward in its drive to democratise access to quality education by founding its own university, the University for Peace, in Costa Rica. Soon after, a new UN international development strategy was devised and approved during the General Assembly's 35th session in December 1980. The 3rd Development Decade, which began on 1 January 1981, prioritised better access to quality education for all (United Nations General Assembly, 1980).

Over the next 20 years, the UN continued to develop its approach to education as central to human development. At the 1995 World Summit for Social Development, which took place in Copenhagen, Denmark, a new consensus was reached on the need to provide access to quality education and the central role it merited (United Nations Department of Economic and Social Affairs, 2023). Signatories committed to achieving universal and equitable access to quality education with a particular focus on addressing inequities related to race, national origin, gender, age or disability. Implementation, in this regard, was to be focused on 'people-centred sustainable development'. Commitment 6 was particularly inclusive and addressed all needs, from basic primary education to lifelong learning opportunities. It also emphasised the need to educate girls and women to bridge gender gaps in primary, secondary, vocational and higher education. Due to its inclusivity and expansive recommendations, it could be argued that SDG 4 is rooted in Commitment 6.

By the time SDG 4 was approved in 2015, significant efforts had been made across the world to address inequalities related to access to quality education. This included work done to build on the 1995 World Summit for Social Development via the Millennium Development Goals (MDGs), whose goals constituted the foundational blocks of SDG 4. The MDGs had a limited timeframe to be a force for change. However, attempts to meet Target 2A of MDG 2, which was aimed at ensuring that children everywhere will be able to complete a full course of primary schooling, resulted in a net increase of primary school enrolments in the Global South, from 83% in 2000 to 91% in 2015. Sub-Saharan African countries registered a 20% increase over the same period, outperforming any other part of the world.

For universities today, the challenges to ensure equitable access to higher education for all are many and significant, but the SDGs serve as a benchmark and a driver. This is evident in the emergence of global education rankings. For example, the Times Higher Education Impact Ranking includes 1,591 universities from 112 countries, and the newly established QS World University Rankings: Sustainability has a pool of more than 700 universities. It is difficult to imagine these ranking systems without the SDGs as a foundation for evaluation.

These ranking systems show that there is a growing number of higher education institutions committed to becoming part of a collective force that attempts to provide broader access to quality education. However, societal engagement, equitable access and opportunities to succeed in education are difficult to measure and do not substantially influence, let alone rival, the power of research metrics. As such, the incentives to strategically embrace, define and measure societal relevance through fair access to education, or by changing the definition of high-quality research, remain challenging.

PRINCIPLES OF ENGAGEMENT

To help universities engage society in ways that are consistent with the principles and outcomes of the SDGs, we require intellectual frameworks that help us think about engagement in robust and meaningful ways. 'Engagement' might instinctively feel good ethically, politically and intellectually. However, it is a term loaded with history, particularly regarding universities and work that has historically been described as 'outreach' or 'service' and, in those ways, not valued. The purpose of this section is to firstly ground the term in a particular history, not because it is the 'correct' history but because it has long been prevalent within a scholarly context that can be accessed and extended by others.

This starting place takes advantage of a particular institutional formation as a resource for thinking about how universities might increase their relevance and enhance their efforts towards making a greater societal impact. That formation is the 'land-grant' university in the United States, a new form of a university organised to promote the common good, initially via the Morrill Act of the US Congress in 1862. The mission of these universities was to teach practical arts and sciences such as agriculture, mining and engineering, but they were also designed to enable working class Americans to access a liberal education.

'Outreach' was fundamental to this type of university. Key to the structure of the entire land-grant system was the establishment of agricultural experiment stations, which can still be found in every state and territory of the USA. Built into the DNA of this institutional form was the obligation to be relevant within society along with developing the mechanisms to do so. Over time, these agriculturally focused experiment stations were supplemented and, in some cases, replaced by services with broader scope, such as education, health and community wellbeing.

Most universities across the world have hierarchical categories to describe academic work and its value. Research sits at the top of the hierarchy, followed by teaching or education. Then, way below, we find work that is understood as service or citizenship. This is, in part, because research outputs are more easily measured than high-quality teaching or outreach/engagement activity. This is also partly because ranking and rewards systems are focused almost exclusively on research and the reputation associated with it. As such, in many institutions, the value gap between research and everything else has widened considerably. To compound the problem, research in these universities often means disciplinary work that does not necessarily have any connection to improving society (though it certainly can). Given this well-known situation, it became necessary to create new categories of value for those engaged in the intellectual work of 'outreach' or 'engagement'.

Unfortunately, engaged work is understood at too many universities as 'service', which is seen as a dead end for a career at a research university. Michigan State University in the USA was the intellectual leader in establishing a scholarly foundation for engaged intellectual work 30 years ago. This work remains foundational today (see, e.g. volume 20 of the *Journal of Higher Education Outreach and Engagement*, 2016).

In the early 1990s, the executive leadership of Michigan State University commissioned work on outreach and engagement to re-ground the university in its land-grant history and values. The primary outcome, a report titled 'University Outreach at Michigan State University: Enabling Knowledge to Serve Society', argued for a notion of outreach that was distinct from service, which was cross-cutting and a mode of scholarship (Provost's Committee on University Outreach, 1993). While the authors recognise diversity, even disagreement, around the concept of 'scholarship', in this context, the committee understood scholarship as a research and teaching activity, as well as a part of service. 'Teaching, research and service are simply different expressions of the scholar's central concern: knowledge and its generation, transmission, application, and preservation'. Consequently, 'outreach has the same potential for scholarship as the other major academic functions of the University'.

The report's key argument – that 'outreach' is a legitimate category of intellectual work – was extended over time by scholars at a few universities in the USA. Significantly, the value of outreach was recognised in its cross-cutting nature. This resulted in a shift at Michigan State University and other institutions, where outreach, *per se*, was considered far less important and valuable than outreach-research, outreach-teaching and outreach-service. In this sense, outreach-research differs from 'disciplinary' research, with the same applying to teaching and service. As such, outreach transforms standard categories of work at the university towards broader and more engaged outcomes.

As the concept and practice of outreach developed, there were two components to 'outreach'. One is its concern with location (i.e. outside the university), and the other is its focus on transformative engagement. The first component is more direct and obvious. Outreach activity is almost by definition beyond the university's walls. The second component, the meaning and value of engagement as transformative or impactful, has been less clear. In fact, over time, outreach and engagement became related but distinct concepts as a function of efforts to measure and value the work.

As Fear and colleagues (2001) write, forms of outreach such as 'technical assistance outreach – practiced as the introduction of change in a recipient system – is profoundly different from outreach as participatory development where local people engage actively in determining their collective future'. They go on to establish substantive differences between the two concepts: 'Reaching out is academy-centred (knowledge from) and unidirectional (to those who benefit)'. To move towards engagement, they argue for the creation an 'engagement interface', or a conceptual and practical function 'where collaborators from the academy and society engage each other. The interface is a dynamic, evolving, and co-constructed space – a collaborative community of inquiry'. This interface has four characteristics: joint construction of purpose, shared norms, unique perspectives and skill applied in practice and shared appraisal of outcomes (pp. 22–27).

There are many different mechanisms to embed engaged practice and principles throughout an organisation as complex as a university. A common path is a centralised system, where a central team at the institution oversees its civic activity and develops frameworks and initiatives for others to engage with and follow (this is the case at Michigan State University). In contrast, a decentralised approach features a network of coordinating hubs across the university, each with specific remits (such as education or research) to drive their work.

The University of Leeds has adopted a decentralised and distributed approach that is rooted in what Lave and Winger (1991) refer to as 'communities of practice'. Here, a network of academics, professional service staff and students are organised to oversee civic activity that is embedded across the university. The approach and power are distributed to each of the network's constituent members who, in turn, have connections out to faculty/students working at the community level. While this approach is potentially unwieldy, it has the clear benefits of drawing on the passion, experience and enthusiasm of all of those who are involved in community engagement and shares the responsibility (and power) among them.

For universities to be most useful to society, they need to become more engaged and structure this type of work in a way that is valued by the institution. If this does not happen, the work will simply not happen. For universities to be relevant partners in helping societies meet collective obligations – to people, the planet, prosperity, peace and partnerships – they need more and better outreach and engagement programmes. To generate this, universities must think differently and put that thinking to practice in systems, structures and processes.

Accordingly, universities need to redefine success and excellence and create reward systems that recognise and incentivise outreach and engagement. They need explicit interfaces. Most academics, whether focused on research or education, or both, will be interested in fully participating in socially relevant activities. However, university structures often stand in the way of achieving this. If outreach and engagement appear unimportant institutionally, there will be little impetus for university staff to focus their efforts in those areas. Engagement is the most transformative concept but is challenging in practice. As such, it needs a clear set of outcomes and a defined path to become embedded in universities' core strategic aims.

GLOBAL ENGAGEMENT AND THE KNOWLEDGE EQUITY NETWORK

Even though various funding avenues have been traditionally used to broaden access to higher education – including government, university and private scholarships, and in some countries, free access – none of these schemes have really gone as far as required. Here, equity of access does not necessarily mean equality of access. Even in those countries where higher education access is free for all, it is usually conditioned by performance at pre-university levels. As a result, potential students from disadvantaged backgrounds are often left behind.

Such a disparaging situation has deep ethical and social consequences. For universities, developing strategies that address these disparities and creating or expanding initiatives that lead to more equitable knowledge-sharing is vital. Building and supporting such strategies is neither cheap nor easy. However, there is an increasing number of universities across the world that have begun conceiving means of redress for the lack of equal access to quality education and all forms of knowledge in general.

The creation of open educational resources is a good example. Even though the transformational reach of these individual efforts is still limited and not truly global, when put together, they offer a clear marker for the direction that these efforts are taking. Here, too, rich universities in the Global North should embrace these efforts, not with the goal of creating an extra source of income, but with the aim of contributing to equitable access to education globally. It should be a feature of their engagement interface.

There are also other ways to move towards fairer and more equitable access to knowledge and quality education. These include the creation of training and capacity-building programmes, often online, which create platforms for the design and use of open educational resources. This can be observed in the way many universities across the world jointly create and disseminate online content that focuses on solving ongoing global challenges. By creating and developing these digital platforms, truly collaborative, transnational networks have been founded and expanded.

Some recent instances of universities adopting measures to tackle these challenges are well known, and new, emerging initiatives continue to appear. The recently published Africa Charter on Transformative Research Collaborations, jointly led by the universities of Cape Town and Bristol, is an example. The charter, which focuses on collaboration between the UK and African partners, identifies the power imbalances that have pervaded collaboration in the past and offers several principles for redress. The charter is a pioneer effort that will hopefully see similar initiatives blossom soon.

By addressing the power imbalances and influence that African scholars and institutions have been regularly subjected to, the charter constitutes a framework for designing and delivering transformative modes of research collaborations. This is aimed at creating a more even context for knowledge generation and dissemination. In the words of Professor Isabella Aboderin, the Perivoli Chair in African Research and Partnerships at the University of Bristol and a key actor in the development of the charter, as cited by Dell (2023), 'fundamental change … [is] required in Global North-Africa research relations'. Aboderin, alongside Professor Divine Fuh of the University of Cape Town, has referred to the current principle underpinning this relationship as one of an 'unidirectional gaze', which 'positions Africa as the subject rather than the investigator' (Dell, 2023). This type of relationship is unsustainable and must be challenged and systemically transformed.

Another case worth mentioning is that of the Library Fund for Fair Open Science, which was created by the Library Open Science Office. This initiative aims to support non-profit forms of open science and explicitly rejects financing of big commercial publishers in favour of open access options (European University Institute, 2023). As part of the project, the Library Open Science Office has also created the Directory of Open Access Journals and the Directory of Open Access Books. This effort is similar to the Scientific Electronic Library Online initiative, a collaborative, open access publishing project led and mostly supported by universities from Brazil and the rest of Spanish-speaking Latin America.

A more recent attempt to champion the global need for open access to knowledge and quality education is the Knowledge

Equity Network (KEN). The network originated because of ongoing collaborations between the universities of Leeds and Pretoria. It was launched in late 2022 and is headquartered at the University of Leeds. The purpose of the network is to expand equitable access to knowledge on a global scale. As such, the network aims to mainstream openness, accessibly and inclusively among learners, leaders, institutions, organisations and individuals who are committed to the fundamental principle of knowledge equity.

To fulfil its mission, KEN has started to bring together key educational stakeholders who share a commitment to take down paywalls that limit production and access to knowledge across the world. By advocating for the expansion of 'equitable access to knowledge across institutions and geopolitical boundaries', KEN has begun transforming the ways in which the creation, sharing and access to knowledge and a quality education have been carried out until now.

Three core principles underpin KEN's activities. Firstly, the network is intrinsically collaborative. By shifting the focus from competition to collaboration, KEN members can partner with other members. Central to this principle is its global dimension, which recognises the inequities that continue to pervade access to knowledge in the Global South, especially when compared to the Global North. The network is also universal. The continuous production and dissemination of knowledge by and among a few privileged parties must be addressed and transformed so that this knowledge becomes accessible to 'all people to be used as widely as possible'. Finally, and crucially, the network is inclusive and sustainable. Knowledge must be produced and shared in an equitable manner and must achieve equitable outcomes. It is not enough to champion more equitable access to knowledge. The production of this knowledge in a sustainable way is just as important for the longevity of these efforts. Fostering a global community that can adapt and evolve should enable the essential task of keeping pace with technological innovations and geopolitical developments. To transform the ways in which we produce and access knowledge, KEN has produced a declaration that captures the 'collective commitment and aspiration' of its signatory members to 'reduce inequality by increasing access to knowledge'. Based on the network's principles, the declaration puts forward several recommendations that could be truly transformative. These recommendations have been made so that real change can take place.

As partners come together and begin working on solutions to effect change, the Declaration should provide the necessary guidance around the best ways to adopt good governance principles to create more equitable environments, where information is openly shared, rather than continuing to be part of transactional relationships. The Declaration also provides network members with a 'cohesive approach to improve equity, diversity and inclusion', while championing the need 'to move away from competition-focused rankings'. Ultimately, the Declaration endorses collaboration as a main pillar for the more equitable global creation and access to knowledge. Lastly, it commits its signatories to wholeheartedly commit to much needed 'open publication and open practices'.

At the time of writing, the Declaration has been signed by numerous higher education institutions, organisations and individuals. Among them, world-leading universities such as the University of Pretoria, Mahidol University, the University of Macau, Nairobi University and the University of Hamburg. Plenty of organisations and individuals have also added their signatures. These include the International Council for Open Distance Education (Sweden), Dagbani Wikimedians User Group (Ghana), the Librarianship Council (Moldova), María Soledad Ramirez-Montoya, Martha Mosha, Nokuthula Mchuni and Peter Suber, among many others.

As KEN expands and more concrete activities are jointly devised and advanced by its members, the recommendations made by signatories of the Declaration should serve as a guide. These recommendations, organised into sets, focus on the most effective ways for KEN members to transform the currently inequitable landscape into one that abides by the network's core principles. Two sets of recommendations are of direct relevance to the purpose of this chapter. These are the general recommendations for higher education and those specific to higher education institutions. The remaining three sets, which relate to funding agencies, publishers and suppliers and individuals, organisations and networks, are shaped in a very similar way to the ones discussed below. Four general recommendations, applicable to all signatories, set the tone. They are:

1. The higher education system must create a culture and environment where there is open and equitable access to research-led education and the benefits of knowledge and innovation that result from higher education.
2. The higher education system must actively address inequalities (social, geographical and financial, among others) that prevent or limit open access to higher education.
3. The higher education system must move away from a competition-based environment to a global collaborative endeavour where partnership is actively sought, celebrated and rewarded.
4. The higher education system must create an environment that respects and supports all knowledge systems, acknowledging their importance and value.

For higher education institutions in particular, the declaration makes nine recommendations. These speak to the very essence of how universities can turn their strengths into a transformative force for good when it comes to creating, accessing and disseminating knowledge. Higher education institutions must:

1. Publish a knowledge equity statement by 2025, incorporating tangible commitments aligned with the principles and objectives below.
2. Commit to institutional action(s) to support a sustained increase of published educational material being open and freely accessible for all to use and reuse for teaching, learning and research.
3. Commit to institutional action(s) to support a sustained increase of new research outputs being transparent, open and freely accessible for all, and which meet the expectations of funders.
4. Use openness as an explicit criterion in reaching hiring, tenure and promotion decisions. Reward and recognise open practices across both research and research-led education. This should include the importance of interdisciplinary and/or collaborative activities and the contribution of all individuals to activities.

5. Define equity, diversity and inclusion targets that will contribute towards open and inclusive higher education practices and report annually on progress against these targets.
6. Create new mechanisms in and between higher education institutions that allow for further widening participation and increased diversity of staff and student populations.
7. Review the support infrastructure for open higher education and invest in the human, technical and digital infrastructure that is needed to make open higher education a success.
8. Promote the use of open interoperability principles for any research or education software/system that you procure or develop, explicitly highlighting the option of making all or parts of content open for public consumption.
9. Ensure that all research data conform to the FAIR Data Principles: 'findable', accessible, interoperable and reusable.

Ultimately, KEN is nothing short of an attempt to push boundaries and move away from needlessly rigid, old-fashioned and perhaps all-too-comfortable models. It attempts to lead the way into a new era of equitable engagement. By placing universities at the forefront of this movement, such a network has provided the means to a more just end, where old ideas and practices can be replaced with new and more equitable ones.

CONCLUSION: ENGAGEMENT INTERFACES MUST BE 'GLOCAL'

The land-grant movement in the USA and the civic university collective in the UK are good examples of how a social mission can be articulated and progressed institutionally in the Global North. In outlining those histories and the notion of an 'engagement interface', this chapter provides one rationale for promoting an 'engaged university'. However, it is just as true that most of the literature and published case examples in civic engagement are also dominated by ideology, cultures and approaches from the Global North. To broaden and enrich our understanding of the university's role in meeting development goals, we need to do more than work locally within frameworks with narrow viewpoints.

As argued here – and as a common thread running through this publication – working alongside institutions in the Global South is critical to ensure local civic work is informed by best practice from different knowledge systems and contexts. Collaboration is a central pillar of such civic work. As such, working with other higher education institutions locally, nationally and internationally serves to enrich a university's trajectory, approach and thinking in its local civic engagement. In other words, to fully live the transformative power of university collaborations to attain the SDGs, particularly SDG 4, we need a layer to our 'engagement interface' that encompasses the 'glocal'.

Generating societal impact is very close to the core role, if not the core role, of universities and the people who work and study in them. This raises the question of why many higher education institutions have not placed this at the top of their strategic agendas. If universities want to be relevant in tackling the huge global challenges that face our planet, social engagement and outreach need to become a more central goal. This is especially so because, in essence, most academics and students are driven by a shared desire to make a real difference in the world. Also, the fundamental pillars of the SDGs – people, planet, prosperity, peace and partnerships – are clearly at the heart of what drives universities. This should open them up to the needs of local and global communities and make them willing and able to drive a research and teaching agenda designed in collaboration with the very populations that could gain the most from the combined work.

Doing so requires a redefinition of excellence and a strategic move towards more generosity and collaboration. The societal mission of universities is underdeveloped, mainly because most systems that measure universities' status and worth are focused on competition and a narrow definition of excellence. If excellence was based on measures of local, regional and ultimately global societal impact, much progress could be made in incentivising universities to pursue these goals. Such engaged work also needs to align closely with a university's strategic outcomes and its key performance indicators. An elite university needs to be understood more as socially impactful.

If we want to truly start addressing the SDGs, it is critical for universities across the world to unite with a shared commitment to progress social justice and civic responsibility at the global and local levels. Our work needs to align with the priorities of local and global partners, in collaboration with key stakeholders, to ensure an ongoing and reflexive approach to responding to community priorities. This is only possible if community stakeholders are part of the work and empowered to help set the agenda.

We are convinced that there is an urgency to put systems and structures in place so that universities can truly realise their power and potential to make a difference to their global and local communities by 2030 (as is required to attain SDG 4). At the same time, we are under no illusions about how challenging it will be to win the argument that excellence is impossible without social impact and the deep collaborations necessary to deliver.

REFERENCES

Dell, S. (2023, March 15). *Bold new charter aims for balance in North-South partnerships*. University World News. https://www.universityworldnews.com/post.php?story=20230315085144945

European University Institute. (2023, July 15). Library fund for fair open science. https://www.eui.eu/Research/Library/PublishingAndOpenScience/EndorsedOpenScienceInitiatives.

Fear, F. F., Rosaen, C. L., Foster-Fishman, P., & Bawden, R. J. (2001). Outreach as scholarly expression: A faculty perspective. *Journal of Higher Education Outreach and Engagement*, 6(2), 21–33.

Lave, J., & Wenger, E. (1991). *Situated learning: Legitimate peripheral participation*. Cambridge University Press.

Provost's Committee on University Outreach. (1993). *University outreach at Michigan State University: Extending knowledge to serve society*. https://engage.msu.edu/upload/documents-reports/Provost CommitteeReport_2009ed.pdf

United Nations. (n.d.a.). *Target 2.A: Ensure that, by 2015, children everywhere, boys and girls alike, will be able to complete a full course of primary schooling*. United Nations. https://www.un.org/millenniumgoals/education.shtml

United Nations Department of Economic and Social Affairs. (2023, July 15). *Copenhagen declaration on social development*. https://www.un.org/development/desa/dspd/world-summit-for-social-development-1995/wssd-1995-agreements/cdosd-introduction.html\

United Nations General Assembly. (1970). *International strategy for the second United Nations development decade*. Twenty-fifth Session. https://documents.un.org/doc/resolution/gen/nr0/348/91/pdf/nr034891.pdf?token=1JEydHJtNCkyiAFF3B&fe=true

United Nations General Assembly. (1980). *International development strategy for the third United Nations development decade*. Thirty-fifth Session. https://documents.un.org/doc/resolution/gen/nr0/390/75/pdf/nr039075.pdf?token=863PZ3y2yVjA2rjISu&fe=true

6

CONCLUSION AND WAY FORWARD: A STRATEGIC FRAMEWORK FOR HIGHER EDUCATION TO ACHIEVE SDG 4 TARGETS

Brian Chicksen

University of Pretoria, South Africa

ABSTRACT

Achieving targets within Sustainable Development Goal (SDG) 4 is key to successfully achieving all the goals within the SDG framework. In this chapter, the role of higher education in attaining SDG 4 is discussed in relation to achieving the other 16 SDGs. This is done by reflecting on the prevailing and anticipated challenges and opportunities faced by the higher education sector and proposing a strategic framework to enable realisation of its full potential. A design-thinking approach to formulating strategy is used.

Within the framework, the intent of global higher education systems as integral to society and societal transformation through their contribution to the accelerated achievement of SDG 4 is articulated. A set of principles guide the framework's implementation, supported by various enablers. Key philosophies within the framework include a shared higher purpose, authentic and transdisciplinary collaboration as equals for mutual benefit and co-creation with innovation to amplify collective impacts. A pathway to impact links philosophical aspects of the framework to tangible and intentional action. It comprises a sequential set of processes that frame and organise subsidiary high-level considerations and focus areas to enable coherence of action.

Keywords: Co-creation; design-thinking approach; next-generation collaboration; strategic framework; transdisciplinary work; transformational change

INTRODUCTION

While much work needs to be done to enhance the higher education sector's collective impact and contribution to achieving SDG 4, there is cause for optimism by means of emerging ideas and concepts. However, beyond optimism, there lies a compelling case for placing the sector at the forefront of advancing a societal agenda for sustainable and inclusive development. Through its very nature, quality education that builds broad societal capability, creates new knowledge and informs the policy landscape is a prerequisite for enhanced life chances. Furthermore, multiple linkages and dependencies between SDG 4 and other goals in the SDG framework exist. As such, attaining SDG 4 gives impetus to achieving the others.

Despite the higher education sector's many flaws and challenges, it is of vital importance for key stakeholders to leverage collective and coherent action within and across it. Once this is achieved, the sector is likely to make a profound impact on actualising a shared future with meaningful existence.

In seeking to advance the conversation, and by drawing on discussions from the previous chapters, this chapter develops a strategic framework for higher education to achieve the SDG 4 targets. To do this, a design-thinking approach is used, which focuses on three aspects (adapted from Rumelt, 2011):

- A synthesis of our current realities: challenges, opportunities and key issues at hand.

- A proposed strategic framework for the higher education sector's response to SDG 4.
- A pathway towards shaping and organising a high-level and coherent set of focus areas.

Important to note is that the design-thinking approach is not based on proof in the quantitative sense. Rather, it is grounded in considered thinking and validity, which seek to demystify and make sense of complexity by using heuristic method (Martin, 2009).

This framework could be used as a preliminary tool to engage diverse partners and audiences and to accelerate collective action for positive change. The rationale for using this approach is to introduce shared philosophies and certain principles at a high level, within the context of a global higher education ecosystem. Positioning content of the framework at this level should enable contextual translation within individual institutions and collaborations.

UNDERSTANDING THE CHALLENGE – THREATS, OPPORTUNITIES AND KEY ISSUES

The complex and multifaceted challenges faced by the higher education sector have been addressed extensively in this book so far. These challenges span geographic and sectoral boundaries and affect diverse societal constituencies differently. They are largely driven by disparities and imbalances in societal ecosystems that act as powerful barriers to innovation and societal reform. Key issues here include limited access to higher education institutions, inadequate resourcing, inequitable provision of quality education, Eurocentric approaches to education, unpreparedness of graduates entering the workplace and uneven opportunities for graduates.

These challenges are not discrete in that they are not limited to a north-south global divide. They are also given expression across and within countries and even within various higher education partnerships. They often intersect with each other, demonstrating linkages and dependencies that amplify the extent of their severity and adverse impacts on society and the environment. An example of the complex and interrelated nature of these challenges can be found in how fragmented educational ecosystems are, along with the competitive stance adopted by higher education institutions collectively, that limit the emergence of holistic and sustainable solutions.

Where resources and capacity are constrained, students who enter the higher education system may not be fully prepared for the rigour of tertiary education and consequently experience lower success rates. Similarly, successful graduates who are not adequately prepared for the workplace have lower earning potential and contribute sub-optimally to economic development and societal transformation. Combining these interconnected risks has the potential to drive a vicious cycle of underperformance, the widening of the knowledge divide and worsening inequality. Perspectives on the democratisation of education are clearly not universally lived and felt, and efforts to reshape global higher education for coherent and intentional impact tend to be uncoordinated.

There are, however, profound opportunities for transformational change. A major one lies in broadening access across generations and geographies, which would lead to widespread knowledge-sharing, a deeper talent pool and more creativity. Bridging the technology divide, leveraging digital transformation and navigating other challenges that emerge from technological advancement will likely enable a dramatic broadening of access to higher education, as well as contribute to advancing the academic project to build capacity and create new knowledge for societal benefit.

The importance of collaboration is foregrounded when societal problems are acknowledged as complex and far reaching. Such collaborations go beyond the higher education sector towards involving multisectoral stakeholders in work that is transdisciplinary. Where collaborations have balanced power relationships that are focused on mutual benefit, indigenous or embedded knowledge is embraced rather than disregarded as inferior. In this situation, complexity is addressed more effectively, and the foundation is laid for more innovative approaches to address the grand challenges facing humanity. Effective partnering, as an extension of collaboration, enables the leveraging of resources and a greater ability to mobilise high-impact and sustainable funding.

The challenges and opportunities discussed here are not exhaustive. They do, however, provide an outline of the higher education

Focusing question 1

How do we broaden inclusivity across all the dimensions of higher education, from access, through the provision of equitable quality education, to expanded post-education life opportunities and lifelong learning?

Focusing question 2

How do we nurture a critical mass of graduates globally to serve as societal agents of transformation in complex and dynamic landscapes, and a rapidly changing world of work?

Focusing question 3

How do we engage more meaningfully – within the sector and more broadly with society – to ensure relevance and amplify our impacts?

Fig. 6.1. Focusing Questions That Shape the Strategic Framework's Design.
Source: Author.

landscape. They also enable the development of three focusing questions that shape the strategic framework's design, as well as a pathway for its application. Fig. 6.1 introduces these questions.

The approaches we take and the extent to which these questions are addressed are likely to play an important part in the evolution and strengthening of the higher education sector. This is especially so when considering the sector's key role in societal transformation through SDG 4. As such, they inform the development of a strategic framework for higher education to achieve SDG 4 targets.

A PROPOSED STRATEGIC FRAMEWORK FOR THE HIGHER EDUCATION SECTOR'S RESPONSE TO SDG 4

The framework's four main aspects are discussed first. This is followed by an outline of the strategic intent of higher education as an agent for societal transformation. A set of guiding principles that underpin the framework and its intent is then provided. Key enablers of the framework are introduced and, lastly, the processes required for the effective implementation of the framework are outlined. A key feature of the proposed framework (Fig. 6.2) is its broad applicability across the higher education sector, which enables a consistent yet relevant approach for different contexts (Chicksen et al., 2018).

Intent

Global higher education ecosystems are integral to society and societal transformation through their contribution to the accelerated achievement of SDG 4.

Principles	Enablers	PATHWAY TO ACTION
The following principles guide the framework's implementation: • As an integral part of society, we aspire to contribute to the public good. • We respond to the grand challenges facing humanity. • We embrace innovation and leverage technology to achieve SDG 4 goals. • We value a plurality of knowledge, seeking inclusivity and broadened access to knowledge. • We actively pursue partnerships and collaboration to co-create initiatives and amplify our impact. • Our partnerships demonstrate equality, dignity and respect.	The following aspects help enable this framework: • An authentic commitment to transformative societal impact. • Sharing a higher order purpose that transcends self and partisan interests. • Identifying and addressing barriers and imbalances across ecosystems. • Recognising and capitalising on opportunities. • Encouraging open education and open science. • Valuing different perspectives and encouraging honest conversations. • Seeking mutual benefit as equal partners with shared risk and shared reward.	The following processes address a pathway to action: 1. Affirming and strengthening a shared philosophy on the transformative role of HE. 2. Embedding the principles into institutional cultures and practices. 3. Establishing multisectoral strategic partnerships. 4. Reshaping work in higher education. 5. Strengthening capability of educators and learners and ensuring quality education. 6. Demonstrating and amplifying impact. 7. Learning with adoption, adaptation and scale.

Fig. 6.2. Proposed Strategic Framework for the Higher Education Sector's Response to SDG 4.
Source: Adapted from Chicksen et al. (2018).

Conclusion and Way Forward

Higher education institutions are an integral part of society and, in owing their existence to society, they should aspire to contribute to the public good. By virtue of their core functions and the work they do, they are well placed to respond to the grand challenges facing humanity, particularly poverty and inequality. Innovation and leveraging technology are essential here and entail broadening access, strengthening quality education and its delivery and enhancing graduate readiness for future career paths.

'Next generation' collaborations and partnerships amplify impact beyond what is possible through an institution working in isolation. Such partnerships entail shifting away from mental models and approaches which perpetuate individualism or structural inequality within partnering arrangements, to valuing all participants and leveraging their diversity (London & Hart, 2011). In transitioning from historic Eurocentric perspectives and power imbalances, relationships between partners and collaborators will be characterised by equality, dignity and respect, valuing a plurality of knowledge and seeking mutual benefit.

To meet the intent of higher education as a critical agent of societal transformation, as given expression through the strategic framework's guiding principles, an enabling set of conditions needs to be nurtured and strengthened. Responding to Brink's provocative challenge to higher education institutions – that we should be asking 'What are we good for?' rather than 'What are we good at?' – requires introspection on how we see ourselves in relation to society (Brink, 2018).

Being an agent of societal transformation requires individual and collaborating institutions to share a higher purpose that transcends individual or partisan interests. This should be coupled with an authentic commitment to leading transformative change that is sustainable. Barriers and imbalances across educational and other societal ecosystems should be actively identified and addressed, while opportunities should be recognised and capitalised on with the requisite flexibility and agility. Central to the democratisation of education is valuing different perspectives, forms and sources of knowledge and advancing open education and open science to expand the richness and accessibility of knowledge for meaningful transformational change.

To be meaningful, it must be relevant to different geographic and cultural contexts. Two-way mutuality that flows from valuing different perspectives must go beyond the concept of shared reward to include the concept of shared risk. Such shared risk is not limited to the idea of economic risk, rather, it acknowledges that all parties have something to offer and should all have some form of binding commitment (London & Hart, 2011).

The higher education sector, and the world, is dealing with seemingly intractable, complex and deep-seated challenges. Putting the framework into action and addressing the focusing questions, thus, require a fundamental shift from adopting traditional and transactional approaches in the way we do things, to being transformational in outlook and action.

To enable the shift, and to help us navigate the complexity, two critical and independent dimensions need to be considered. These are the levels of trust and the quality of relationships between relevant stakeholders, and the quality of the solutions that are brought to bear. Each dimension has two extreme positions, and their relatively independent nature allows the formation of a 2 × 2 matrix, as shown in Fig. 6.3 (Chicksen et al., 2018).

The transactional space is characterised by low levels of trust and the application of constrained solutions. People and groups work in silos and may have self or partisan interests. Conflicts are addressed through negotiation where the outcomes are commonly trade-offs or zero-sum games with winners and losers.

The transformational space, on the other hand, is characterised by high levels of trust, and the development of solutions that are creative and innovative. A transformational approach is suited to complexity and to addressing 'wicked problems'. It requires collaboration, co-design and co-creation, and the desired outcome is multiple streams of value – value protected and new value created – as complex challenges are addressed. Value is protected when risks are managed better to prevent adverse impacts, while new value is created when ideas and innovations capitalise on opportunities for societal upliftment (International Council on Mining and Metals, 2024).

The shift from being transactional to transformational calls for a two-pronged approach that entails strengthening levels of trust

Conclusion and Way Forward

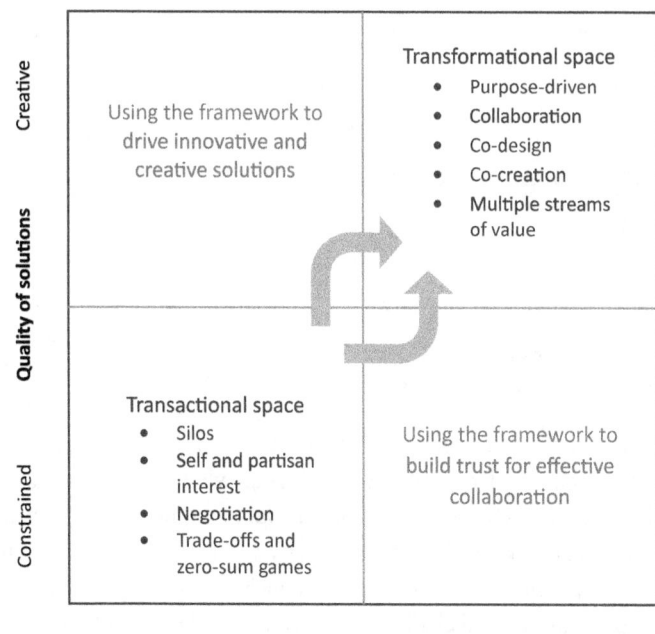

Fig. 6.3. A Two-pronged Approach to Shift from Being Transactional to Being Transformational (University of Pretoria, 2020).

and the quality of relationships and enabling the development of innovative and creative solutions. This thinking is given expression through the framework.

A PATHWAY TO IMPACT FOR ORGANISED AND COHERENT ACTION

The pathway to impact links philosophical aspects of the framework to tangible and intentional action. It comprises a sequential set of processes that frame and organise subsidiary high-level considerations and focus areas to enable coherence of action. In the spirit of continuous learning and improvement, the pathway is iterative (Chicksen et al., 2018). The connected nature of the steps in the pathway is shown in Fig. 6.4.

To have transformational societal impacts, we must first transform ourselves. This includes a reflection on what it means to be

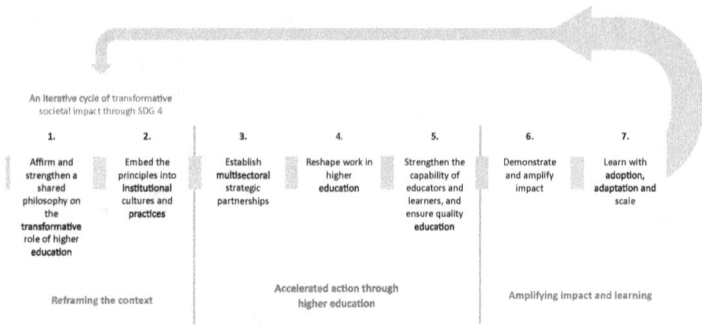

Fig. 6.4. Pathway to Impact.
Source: Adapted from Chicksen et al. (2018).

an integral part of society in relation to the institution's context, constituencies and aspirations. Exploring what we are good for seeks to bring a convergence of institutional strengths and societal needs. Considerations include inclusivity and broadening access, the nature of the institution and its distinguishing competences and the most pressing societal challenges in its context. This enables focused and intentional responsiveness to prioritised societal challenges without seeking to be all things to all people or reducing distinctive identity and capabilities between individual institutions. Notably, the diversity and complementarity of competences are likely to be good for the higher education sector as a whole. At the same time, it is a necessary step towards re-establishing and strengthening trust between the higher education sector and society at large.

The process of reflection and exploration serves to set direction. Effective change management is then needed to socialise the direction, embed the principles into the institutional culture, and nurture commitment for enduring change and responsiveness. Embedding key principles such as collaboration, co-design and innovation sets the institution up for subsequent steps of the pathway.

Establishing strategic partnerships is increasingly being recognised as critical to strengthening the capacity of the higher education sector and amplifying desired impacts. As this trend progresses, it is likely that the dynamics of competition within the higher education sector will change, with the ability to collaborate and form meaningful partnerships becoming a powerful source of distinctive capability (Prahalad & Ramaswamy, 2004). Such partnerships will not only seek to address power imbalances within the higher education ecosystem but will value and embrace different sources and forms of knowledge and extend to different sectors beyond higher education. Advancing open science and open education along with increased collaboration and partnering activities will have the dual effect of further democratising education, and achieving impact at the community level, where it is needed most.

Key outcomes of this new approach to partnering and collaboration for mutual benefit are the ongoing transformation of participants in these initiatives and reshaping work within the sector. This cuts across the core functions of teaching, learning, research and engagement. The processes of co-designing initiatives, innovating, widening perspectives of knowledge, knowledge-sharing and pursuing societal relevance must inevitably inform the academic project, from curriculum renewal to new modes of teaching, research, community engagement and assessment.

The combination of disruptions in the environment outside the higher education landscape, advances in technology and learning from each other will continue to drive innovations in higher education. These will need to be harnessed for continuous and step-change improvements in quality education and the protection or creation of value. The latter is seen when there are strengthened capabilities in higher education institutions, educators, researchers and learners on the higher education journey. Such individual and collective capabilities are a key source of transformative societal impact.

A reimagined philosophy and coherent set of actions enable us to demonstrate the difference that we make in society. This is critical to positioning higher education as central to the aspirations of SDG 4 and a key contributor to the attainment of the other SDGs.

Recognising the limitations of current approaches that evaluate impact, our work ahead entails developing new baskets of qualitative and quantitative metrics. Key aspects of 'next generation' impact metrics include being able to navigate the complexities associated with grand and systemic societal challenges, understanding attributable impact from a plethora of initiatives driven by different players and concurrently under way and assessing impact through the lenses of targeted participants' and recipients' experiences.

In the spirit of lifelong learning, we recognise that we need to learn individually as institutions and collectively as a sector. This process of learning is iterative and is particularly relevant in a world where the complexities we face are dynamic and continue to evolve and where frequent disruptions have become the norm. The way we build such capabilities for continual responsiveness is an essential contribution to creating the conditions for a critical mass of populations to thrive and reach their full potential. In this iterative process of learning, we embrace multiple forms and sources of knowledge and have experiences that provoke questions and reflections. These, in turn, stimulate new insights that generate ideas about solutions that need to be tested. Implementing these solutions will provide new knowledge and experiences for a virtuous cycle of learning.

CONCLUDING REMARKS

SDG 4 is an enabler and catalyst for attaining the other SDGs, making it a critical component of the SDG framework. Notwithstanding the daunting nature of the grand challenges facing humanity, as part of a broader educational ecosystem, higher education has the profound potential to accelerate the achievement of SDG 4 targets by 2030.

To fully realise this potential, significant shifts are needed in the higher education sector in terms of its structural and systemic drivers and constituent institutions. These include addressing imbalances and inequalities across the sector and moving towards collaborative rather than individualistic approaches. Given the current fragmented nature of higher education, these changes cannot be prescribed or forced. Rather, what is likely to emerge from a reimagined philosophy and the processes that follow is a sector that is driven to make collective and beneficial societal impact.

This book seeks to advance discussions around the higher education sector's role in attaining SDG 4. As such, it presents thematic and forward-looking approaches to help us achieve equal and inclusive development. In this concluding chapter, a proposed framework and pathway to impact are presented. These provide a structure for dialogue, while enabling the content of conversations to be developed by participants for relevance in their contexts. By strengthening a shared purpose and broadly consistent approach without constraining innovation and creativity, we can contribute to addressing imbalances, furthering coherence and amplifying collective impact across the sector.

As we reflect on the future of our sector and the world we share, we realise that significant changes must occur from within for us to have meaningful impacts beyond our immediate boundaries. The extent to which we evolve and are responsive to societal changes and challenges will determine the extent to which we secure our future – as institutions, as a sector and as a society.

REFERENCES

Brink, C. (2018). *The soul of a University*. Bristol University Press.

Chicksen, B., Cole, M., Broadhurst, J., Meyer, H., Hoffman, A., & Viljoen, D. (2018). *Embedding the sustainable development goals into business strategy and action*. MtM & MilA Working Paper 1, University of Cape Town. Cape Town. https://thevault.exchange/?get_group_doc=143/1553857838-EmbeddingtheSDGgoalsintothebusinessstrategy.pdf

International Council on Mining and Metals. (2024). *Financial valuation tool for sustainability investments. ICMM guidance*. ICMM. London. https://guidance.miningwithprinciples.com/case_study/financial-valuation-fv-tool-for-sustainability-investments/

London, T., & Hart, S. (2011). *Next generation business strategies for the base of the pyramid* (2nd ed.). Pearson Education, Inc.

Martin, R. (2009). *The design of business: Why design thinking is the next competitive advantage*. Harvard Business School Publishing.

Prahalad, C. K., & Ramaswamy, V. (2004). *The future of competition: Co-creating unique value with customers*. HBS Press.

Rumelt, R. (2011). *Good strategy/bad strategy: The difference it makes and why it matters*. Profile Books Ltd.

University of Pretoria. (2020). *UP 2019 sustainable development report*. University of Pretoria.

LIST OF CONTRIBUTORS

Manuel Barcia — Leeds University, UK
Patrick Effiong Ben — The University of Manchester, UK
Dawie Bornman — University of Pretoria, South Africa
Simone Buitendijk — University of Salford, UK
Samantha Castle — University of Pretoria, South Africa
Brian Chicksen — University of Pretoria South Africa
Lisa Coleman — Adler University, USA
Willem Fourie — Stellenbosch University, South Africa
Monroe France — Tufts University, USA
Jeffrey Grabill — Leeds University, UK
Sonia Kumar — Leeds University, UK
Tawana Kupe — University of Pretoria, South Africa
Emmanuel Manyasa — Usawa Agenda, Kenya
Teboho Moja — New York University, USA
Ramola Ramtohul — University of Mauritius, Mauritius
Palesa Vuyolwethu Tshandu — New York University, USA
Gerald Wangenge-Ouma — University of Pretoria, South Africa

INDEX

Advancing SDG 4 through education justice interventions, 64–69
Africa Charter on Transformative Research Collaborations, 105
African Union Commission (AUC), 60
African Union's Agenda 2063, 83
African universities, 69
Agenda for Sustainable Development (2030), 91
Artificial intelligence (AI), 17–18

Basic education, 59–60, 64
Bilateral partnerships, 21
Black American students, 47
Black students, 47
Blended learning, 68
Broadening access, 39, 116, 119, 122
Broadening engagement, 11, 96–109
Building capability for impact, 11, 76–91

Canada West Foundation, 25
Capacity, 116
Catastrophic events, 77
ChatGPT, 27
Civic university, 109
Climate change, 18
Co-creation, 24, 120
Co-designing, 6, 9, 123
Coherent action, pathway to impact for, 121–124

Coherent set of actions, 123
Collaboration, 29, 110, 116
    engaged responsiveness through, 7–8
Collaborative efforts, 9
Colour-blind government strategies, 47
Communities of practice, 103
Community engagement programmes, 67
Continuing education and training (CET), 26
Copernicus Climate Change Service, 76
COVID-19 pandemic, 42, 62–63, 68
Critical competence, 83
Cultural gender norms in higher education institutions, 44
Cultural knowledge, 28–29
Curriculum renewal and transformation, 123
Cybersecurity, 17

Decolonial methodologies in education, 24
Decolonised education, 24
Democratic systems, 3
Design-thinking approach, 115
Digital divide, 3, 20, 23
Digital platforms, 23
Digital transformation, 19
Diminished government funding, 39
Disability, 46–47
Diversification in higher education, 14

Index

Dominant higher education strategy in the West, 39
Dominant representation, 22

Economic diversification, 27
Ecosystem resilience, 8
Education
　disability, 46–47
　equal opportunities in, 10
　exclusionary factors, 42
　gender, 44–46
　race and ethnic minority groups, 47–48
　social class, 42–44
　universities and challenges in neoliberal era, 38–42
Education ecosystems, 14
Education injustice, 60–64
　in higher education, 60
Education justice, 57–60
　advancing SDG 4 through education justice interventions, 64–69
Educational credentials, 28
Educational exclusion, 11, 55–57
Educational mission of universities, 41
Educational processes, 36
Engagement
　interfaces, 102, 109–111
　and outreach, 9, 110
　principles, 100–103
Epistemic oppression, 63–64
Equal opportunities, 36–48
Equality, 35–36, 57, 104, 119
Equitable global partnerships, 10
Ethnic minority groups, 47–48
Eurocentric approaches to global education challenges, 21
Eurocentric education, 21
Exclusion from learning phenomenon, 61
Exclusionary approach, 46

Finalisation process, 84
Financial resources, 62

Gender, 44–46
　gap in higher education, 44
　and gender injustice, 56
　gender-biased norms and stereotypes, 45
　gender-biased socialization, 45
　representation, 66
Global Association of MDP, 84–85
Global economic system, 19
Global education ecosystems, 7
　recent developments and challenges in, 18–20
　rethinking partnerships to achieve SDG 4 targets, 20–27
　SDG 4 and, 15–18
　strategic partnerships for delivery of SDG4 in, 10
　student perspective on implementation of SDG 4, 27–30
Global engagement and knowledge equity network, 104–109
Global government practices, 20
Global North, 7, 9, 17, 27, 29–30
Global partnerships, 24
Global South, 7, 9, 17, 28–29
Global sustainability challenges, 78
Government-subsidised university education, 39

Health sciences module, 84
Higher education, 2, 14–15, 27, 42, 61
　achieving SDG 4, 10
　broadening engagement and societal responsiveness, 11
　building capability for impact, 11
　creating leverage in reimagined university, 5–6
　engaged responsiveness through collaboration, 7–8
　equal opportunities in education, 10

Index

grand challenges facing humanity, 1–4
institutions, 4, 38, 108, 119
landscape, 65, 123
reimagined role of universities as agents for public good, 4–5
strategic approach to navigating dynamics, addressing barriers and taking opportunities, 8–9
strategic framework for higher education to achieve SDG 4 targets, 12
strategic partnerships for delivery of SDG4 in global education ecosystem, 10
system, 7, 36, 108–116
Higher education sector, 3, 114, 117, 120
strategic framework for higher education sector's response to SDG 4, 117–121
Higher Education Strategy Associates, 29
Historically disadvantaged institutions (HDIs), 65
Development Grant, 65
Humanity, grand challenges facing, 1–4

Impact, 3, 8, 11
Inclusive culture, 46
Inclusive education, 37
Inclusivity, 37, 46
Indigenous knowledge systems, 23
Individual leaders, 8
Inequality, 36
  in higher education sector, 40
  in society, 56
Information and communication technology (ICT), 37, 62
Injustices in basic education, 64
Innovation, 5, 16, 18, 66, 123
Institutional inequality, 41

Institutions of higher learning, 4
Intentional reciprocity, 22
Interconnected risks, 116
Interdisciplinary collaboration, 18, 81
International Association for the Evaluation of Educational Achievement, 61
International Commission on Education for Sustainable Development Practice, The, 78, 80, 82
International partnerships, 22–23
International-developed programmes, 21
Internationalisation, 29
Interuniversity global health partnerships, 22

Joint Research Centre (JRC), 79–80
JuniorTukkie programme, 67

Kenya's basic education system, 61
Key competences, 80
Knowledge equity, 106, 108
Knowledge equity network (KEN), 105–106, 109
  global engagement and, 104–109
Knowledge sharing, 2, 6, 116, 123

Land-grant movement, 109
Leadership competence, 83
Lesbian, gay, transexual, queer and intersex (LGBTQI), 45
Leverage in reimagined university, 5–6
Library Fund for Fair Open Science, 105
Library partnerships, 23
Lifelong learning, 124

MacArthur Foundation, 78
Machine learning, 17
Mahidol University, 107

Massive open online courses (MOOCs), 69
Master's in Business Administration degree (MBA degree), 88
Master's in Commerce degree (MCom degree), 88–89
Master's in Development Practice (MDP), 11, 80–88
Master's in Philosophy degree (MPhil degree), 88
Michigan State University, 101–102
Micro-aggression, 45
Millennium Development Goals (MDGs), 99
Minority groups, 46
Multidisciplinary competence, 83
Multi-faculty MDP programme, 82
Muslim-majority countries, 22

Nairobi University, 107
Neoliberal education policies, 39
Neoliberal era, role of universities and challenges in, 38–42
Neoliberal transformation of higher education sector, 47
Next generation collaborations, 119
Next-Generation University, 8

Online learning, 68
Online teaching, 68
Open educational resources, 104
Open Science, 105, 119
Optimism, 114
Organisation for Economic Cooperation and Development (OECD), 26
Organised action, pathway to impact for, 121–124
Outreach, 100
   concept and practice of, 102
   policies, 43

Participant reflections, 86
Partnership-developed programmes, 21
Partnerships, 17–18, 21, 27, 30
Pay walls, 2
Pedagogical approaches, 81
People with disabilities, 46
People-centred approach, 24, 27
Philosophical modelling, 22
Planet-centred approach, 24, 27
Policies of Western universities, 22
Political dispensations, 56
Post COVID-19 era, 41
Postcolonial learning process, 25
Postgraduate programmes, 79
Practical competence, 83
Pre-University Academy (PUA), 68
Primary goods, 59
Progress in International Reading Literacy Study, 61
Public good, reimagined role of universities as agents for, 4–5
Public higher education systems, 39

Quality education, 56 (see also Higher education)
   in Global South, 27

Race, 47–48
Reciprocal partnerships, 25
Reciprocity-based partnerships, 23
Recognition, 17
Reimagined philosophy, 123
Reimagined university
   functions, 5
   leverage in, 5–6
Renowned academics, 41
Resources, 116
Responsiveness through collaboration, engaged, 7–8
Rethinking partnerships to achieve SDG 4, 20–27
Robotics, 17

Index

Science, technology, engineering and mathematics (STEM), 22, 29, 68
Shanghai's Municipal Education Commission, 59
Sibusiso Bengu Development Programme, 65
Silo-driven approach, 5
Social class, 42–44
Social justice, 58
　approach, 46
　education model, 59
Social reforms, 20
Social sciences module, 84
Social transformation, 17–18, 27
Societal mission of universities, 110
Societal transformation, 119
South African government, The, 65
State subsidies, 40
Steering committee's conceptual work, 82
Strategic approach to navigating dynamics, addressing barriers and taking opportunities, 8–9
Strategic framework for higher education
　challenge, 115–117
　pathway to impact for organised and coherent action, 121–124
　proposed strategic framework for higher education sector's response to SDG 4, 117–121
Strategic initiatives, 29
Strategic partnerships, 23, 122
Students, 60
　with disabilities, 46
　in Global South, 28
　perspective on implementation of SDG 4–27–30
　reflection, 86–87
Substantial social challenges, 77
Supervisor reflection, 87–91
Sustainability education, 80
Sustainable development, 3, 27, 78, 86

Sustainable Development Goal 4 (SDG 4), 1, 4–5, 30, 36, 91, 99, 114
　achieving SDG 4, 10
　advancing SDG 4 through education justice interventions, 64–69
　broadening engagement and societal responsiveness, 11
　building capability for impact, 11
　creating leverage in reimagined university, 5–6
　education injustice, 60–64
　education justice, 57–60
　engaged responsiveness through collaboration, 7–8
　equal opportunities in education, 10
　and global education ecosystem, 15–18
　grand challenges facing humanity, 1–4
　proposed strategic framework for higher education sector's response to, 117–121
　reimagined role of universities as agents for public good, 4–5
　rethinking partnerships to achieve SDG 4 targets, 20–27
　strategic approach to navigating dynamics, addressing barriers and taking opportunities, 8–9
　strategic framework for higher education to achieve SDG 4 targets, 12
　strategic partnerships for delivery of SDG4 in global education ecosystem, 10
　student perspective on implementation of, 27–30

Sustainable Development Goals
(SDGs), 1, 12, 77, 96,
110–111
  SDG 3, 16
  SDG 5, 44
  SDG 8, 16
  SDG 9, 16
  SDG 10, 36
  SDG 17, 17
  universities and, 97–100

Technical and vocational
education and
training (TVET), 66
Technical assistance outreach, 102
Technological advancements, 3
Tertiary institutions, 2
Theoretical competence, 83
Times Higher Education Impact
Ranking, 99
Transactional silos, 6
Transactional space, 120
Transdisciplinarity, 6
Transdisciplinary agenda, 9
Transformation, 2, 14
Transformational approaches, 120
Transformational change, 116
Transformational societal impacts,
121
Transformational space, 120
Trust-based relationships, 6
Tuks Leadership and Individual
Programme (TULIP),
67

Udemy, 69
UNESCO, 14–16
  Global Education Monitoring
Report, 25
Unfair pricing mechanisms, 2

UNICEF, 60
United Arab Emirates, 22
United Nations (UN), 1, 97
Universities, 8, 78, 96–97, 103
  as agents for public good, 4–5
  approach to refocusing
university education,
78–81
  and challenges in neoliberal era,
38–42
  and SDGs, 97–100
University for Peace, 98
University of Hamburg, 107
University of Leeds, The, 103
University of Macau, the, 107
University of Nairobi, 63
University of Pretoria (UP), 67,
107
  approach to refocusing
university education,
78–81
  developmental challenges in
complex world, 76–78
  localising MDP Programme,
81–86
  master's in development
practice at, 11
  participant reflections, 86
  student reflection, 86–87
  supervisor reflection, 87–91

Vocational training, 37

Western-based higher education
institution, 28
World Bank's Groundswell report,
77
World Summit for Social
Development (1995),
98–99

www.ingramcontent.com/pod-product-compliance
Lightning Source LLC
Chambersburg PA
CBHW061942220426
43662CB00012B/2000